HOW TO WORK II

Other titles in preparation

Work in an Office

Sheila Payne

TDipT TDipWP

IRENE'S LEAVING PRESENT?
WHO'S IRENE?

I AM!

How To Books

British Library cataloguing-in-publication data
A catalogue record for this book is available from the British Library.

Copyright © Sheila Payne 1993

First published in 1993 by How To Books Ltd, Plymbridge House,
Estover Road, Plymouth PL6 7PZ, United Kingdom. Tel: Plymouth
(0752) 735251/695745. Fax: (0752) 695699. Telex: 45635.

Typeset by Concept Typesetting Ltd., Salisbury, Wiltshire.
Printed and bound by The Cromwell Press, Broughton Gifford,
Melksham, Wiltshire.

Preface

Some people think working in an office is easy. The picture of a dippy blond, sitting in nice warm surroundings, drinking tea while she files her nails, is still sometimes used on TV and in films to depict the office worker. Most office workers wish it were that simple!

The amount of paperwork generated by even the smallest office is vast and has to be dealt with professionally. Despite the introduction of the computer—which didn't quite have the devastating effect of reducing staff as we were led to believe it would—the most important resource in the office is still the office worker.

I hope this book will portray typical office environments and prepare the reader for what to expect when they start work. It hopes to show young people and returners how they can make a good contribution to their office and how they can learn from their experiences.

Practical information regarding job seeking, interviews and starting work on day one are also covered, as are typical tasks which have to be undertaken regularly. A sample of job descriptions will help you to gain an understanding of the variety of office jobs available.

Written specifically for young people who would like to work in an office and for adults who want to return to office work, it is based on my own experience of working in a variety of offices, and of teaching and counselling young people in office skills over the past seven years.

I would like to thank my family, friends and trainees for their help and support in producing this book, and in particular Shaun, Kellie and Cécile, my artists and proofreaders.

Sheila Payne

Contents

List of Illustrations

1
The World of Office Work

COULD YOU WORK IN AN OFFICE?

Every trade in Britian generates paperwork and someone has to deal with it. Whether it's a small firm with only the owner on the payroll, or a large company employing thousands of people, someone has to pay the bills, fill in tax returns and deal with customers! But there are right and wrong ways of dealing with customers.

Some people have worked in offices for years but don't appear to enjoy their work. They moan and groan when asked to carry out a task and can be unpleasant to the very people they should treat with more respect—their customers. The worst thing about this type of office worker is that he or she really believes they are doing a good job. They turn up on time, have never taken a day off sick and they get through their work.

This book aims to guide you in becoming a genuinely good office worker, someone who is not Superwoman/Superman but a pleasant personality who carries out a job of work to the best of their ability and remembers that the customer is their bread and butter.

Here are two situations which could occur in a typical office environment—one shows the wrong way to deal with customers and the other shows the right way.

The wrong approach

You go to an office to pay a bill only to be greeted by a grumpy clerk. 'Yea?' she/he asks, glaring at you because you have interrupted tea break. Fumbling with your bill you nervously hand over your money dropping small change on the floor.

'I'd like to settle my account.'

Impatiently she/he asks, 'I need your bill—or don't you want a receipt?' As you humbly grunt 'yes' and hand over your invoice, she/he receipts it and throws it back to you across the Reception desk.

'Thanks' you mutter as you walk away—she/he hasn't heard you because they are now reading a magazine. You make a mental note to either pay by cheque next time and send it by post or to write a complaint to the company.

The right approach

You go into an office to pay a bill and are greeted by a smiling clerk. 'Can I help you?' she/he asks pleasantly moving a teacup to the side of the desk.

You hand over your bill and cash. 'I'd like to pay this please,' you say smiling back, even though you're parting with money.

'Thank you, I'll just receipt it for you,' she/he says after counting your money. The bill is handed back to you. 'There you are. See you again,' they say to you as you leave the office. You make a mental note about how pleasant she/he was and how nice it is to be dealt with by someone who knows how to treat a customer.

BEING PERSONALLY EFFECTIVE

Not everyone who works in an office is personally effective. That is, able to handle themselves well and be competent and efficient in their performance. This book aims to help people seeking work in an office environment to become personally effective—people who have not previously worked or have decided to go back to work after bringing up a family. It aims to be realistic in its approach to an ordinary office of the 1990s and covers both large and small office situations.

- It gives realistic qualification requirements for an ordinary person seeking a normal office job, the experience you will need and where you can get it from and how to go about getting your first office job.

- It gives tips on what to do and what not to do when you first enter the office and covers starting work and how to survive, whether you work on your own or with others.

- It gives you a basic run-down on office duties and how to carry them out. It also lists a variety of office equipment found in most offices today and job descriptions for several positions.

- Finally it reflects back on the previous chapters and looks forward to your future as well as listing books you may want to use for reference.

IS OFFICE WORK RIGHT FOR YOU?

Working in an office can be a varied and interesting career. Your duties may bring you into direct contact with the public or you may work alone in a small back room.

Whichever sort of office work you would like to be involved in, firstly you must be honest with yourself about the type of person you are.

For example, if you are an outgoing type who likes to meet people you should think very carefully about a job which involves no contact with the general public. You may be on your own for the majority of the day and your need to socialise could distract you from working. If you are shy and prefer not to meet the public at all, you would be mis-placed to work on a busy reception desk.

With experience, you may find your confidence has grown and you can try your hand at another type of work. You are learning all the time—take advantage of the chance to gain experience in a variety of situations. Before long you will be willing to take on tasks which once appeared daunting to you.

An example of this is answering the telephone. For the inexperienced office worker this can cause instant blood rushes to the face and a palpitating heartbeat, not to mention shaking hands as you try desperately to write down a message. However, within a few days or weeks, this once-dreaded task becomes just another job carried out with ease and confidence.

Office work is challenging and satisfying. You can come into contact with interesting and knowledgeable people and learn a great deal from them. But as in any job, it can at times be frustrating. Working in an office means you may have to keep your cool when you want to explode, or pacify irate customers when they have been waiting two weeks for your electrician to put in urgently required sockets. When you have dealt successfully with your first real problem, you will understand how satisfying office work can really be.

Self-assessment quiz

It is always important to take time to look at yourself and how you dealt with a certain situation. Did you deal with it successfully? Did you feel that you would deal with it differently if it happened again. Looking at your performance honestly and making changes if necessary is called self-assessment and the following quiz is to help get you into work mode. Put yourself into the following office situations and ask yourself how you would deal with each one.

SELF-ASSESSMENT QUIZ

1 Your employer has just rushed into the office as you are about to leave for lunch with a friend. He asks you to type up an urgent quotation which he needs in 10 minutes. Do you:

   (a) Say, 'Sorry, I'm just going to lunch,' and walk out of the office.

   (b) Ask if it can wait until after lunch. If not ask your friend to wait and type it up grudgingly.

   (c) Delay your lunch for 10 minutes because you know it must be important. Get your friend to make a cup of tea.

2 An irate customer has telephoned. She's just received a red reminder for a bill she has already paid. Do you:

   (a) Tell her she hadn't paid when the reminder was sent.

   (b) Tell her you don't know anything about it but will look into it.

   (c) Explain it is a matter of policy to send out reminders and apologise for any inconvenience caused. Tell her you will send a receipt as soon as you receive her cheque.

3 You are taking a photocopy of your favourite pop star and the copier jams. You manage to retrieve the picture but the machine no longer works. Do you:

   (a) Pretend nothing has happened and look surprised when the next person to use it finds it is out of action.

   (b) Vow never to use the photocopier again for your own use but still not tell anyone about the copier's breakdown.

   (c) Vow never to use the photocopier again and then find another member of staff. Tell them what has happened so they can check whether the breakdown requires an engineer or not.

4 You have just taken a phone call from a customer. They have asked you to get your employer to call them back but you have forgotten to ask for their phone number. You only caught the end of their name. Do you:

   (a) Pretend the phone call never happened. They're bound to call back if your boss doesn't return their call.

(b) Scribble out a message with the name you thought they gave you, hoping your boss will know who they are.

(c) Search through the files and customer names to see if any have similiar names. If you have no luck, apologise to your employer on his return. Give him as much information as you can and tell him you won't let it happen again . . . and make sure it doesn't.

5   It's your birthday next week and your friends have decided to take you to a nightclub. As it's on a Wednesday evening do you:

(a) Decide to go off sick on the Thursday so you can have a lie-in.

(b) Tell your boss you've got a doctor's appointment next Thursday and ask if you can come into work after lunch.

(c) Book a day's holiday.

Hopefully your answers will all be (c)s—try not to practise (b)s and definitely leave out the (a)s. If you practise the (a) policy your boss will soon get to know he can't rely or trust you. No matter how smart you think you are, it only takes a short while for people to see through your excuses.

Now try the following small test to see if you can carry out instructions accurately within a certain time. Give yourself two minutes to complete the sheet in fig. 1.

When you have finished the sheet, continue reading.

Can you follow instructions? *Read instruction 15 again carefully.* Have you carried out this instruction? If you have, well done.

Throughout your office career you will need to continually follow instructions carefully—from verbal instructions from your employer to reading instruction manuals for your computer. Always double-check instructions to make sure they are clear in your mind before you action them.

If you carried out any of the tasks in addition to instructions 1 and 2 without reading the rest of the sheet first, you will need to learn to be patient. Take your time and make sure you understand both verbal (spoken) and written instructions before acting on them. That bit of extra time taken to read through and digest information may save you hours of wasted energy.

Example
Justin's employer has just bought a new computer and has asked him to set it up, and hands him an instruction book to help him.

FOLLOWING INSTRUCTIONS

NAME . . . .

DATE . . . .

1   Fill in your name in the space provided at the top of this sheet.

2   Fill in today's date but do nothing else until you have read the rest of the instructions.

3   Underline the heading 'FOLLOWING INSTRUCTIONS'.

4   Write your date of birth at the bottom right-hand corner of the sheet.

5   Underline the date that you have just written.

6   Write your mother's maiden name at the bottom left-hand corner of the sheet.

7   Underline the date that you have just written.

8   Underline the word 'Underline' in questions 3 and 5.

9   Fill in the date at the top of your sheet in the space provided.

10   Draw a circle around your date of birth previously written at the bottom right-hand corner of the sheet.

11   If you are single write a capital 'S' at the top right-hand corner of the sheet. If you are married write a capital 'M'. If you are divorced write a capital 'D'.

12   You are near to the end of this instruction sheet—place a tick by instruction 2.

13   Draw a line under instruction 2.

14   Re-read instruction 2 again—have you carried out its instruction?

15   Do nothing to the sheet apart from carrying out instructions 1 and 2.

Fig. 1. Can you follow instructions accurately?

'It won't print, Mr Geering,' he complains, after trying a test print. 'You'll have to send it back.'

Mr Geering looks at the operating manual. 'Did you take out the pin holding the print head?' he asks.

A red-faced Justin looks closely at the print head. A small pin is anchoring it to the side of the casing. After removing the pin he tries the printer again—and it works perfectly!

WHAT WILL I HAVE TO DO?

If you are starting out in office work, be prepared to begin at the bottom. Go in with your eyes wide open and accept you will probably be the person who has to fetch and carry—'I need these invoices photocopied and posted in five minutes!' 'We need some more milk!' 'Can you pop up the shop . . . *now*?'

Tasks such as making the tea, filing and clearing up behind the boss are the norm together with typing and answering the phone. Lengthy business lunches and trips abroad are probably in the far distant future, if they ever appear at all. But be patient and work hard and once you have proved your worth, who knows where it will lead!

On first joining a company you will not be expected to know everything and everybody. Therefore, it is vitally important you *ask* if you are unsure of something. For instance, if you are filing a document and put it in the wrong file, you could cause untold problems; if the document is urgently required to help sort out a telephone enquiry, its incorrect filing can cost both money and time, not to mention frayed tempers. Therefore, *double-check*.

After a few weeks you should be familiar with the company and no longer need help with basic tasks. If you are still not familiar with the basic systems you may find your colleagues have run out of patience with you—they have jobs to do and if filing is your job you should ensure you know how to do it properly within a few weeks.

THE PERSONAL QUALITIES YOU NEED

- **Be reliable**

Good timekeeping and regular attendance are vital qualities for every office worker. If there is no one available to answer the telephone or type up invoices, the system will soon grind to a halt. If you are genuinely ill—not just hung-over from a trip to the local pub the night before—phone your employer as early as possible so they can arrange for someone to cover for you. If you think you are going to be off sick for more than one day, let them know.

Don't take a whole day off just for a trip to the doctor or dentist—most appointments (including waiting time) should be no longer than an hour. Allow yourself two hours maximum unless you know your treatment will last longer.

If you have a family problem don't use this as an excuse for a day off. Be honest with your employer and explain you may be a bit off colour because you have something on your mind. Only take time off if you genuinely see no other way out of the situation.

● Have confidence—know your business

At the start, everything will be new and you will probably be nervous about answering the 'phone and dealing with customers. Confidence will develop with knowledge—make it your business to gain that knowledge about your company.

● Be helpful

Assess a situation and try to help in any way you can. First impressions of a company are often gained from someone answering the 'phone or sat at the reception desk. If that person is you, then your company's reputation can hinge on how you deal with customers.

● Be cheerful and friendly

Try to be cheerful and friendly to customers both in person and on the 'phone. But don't be too friendly or over-familiar, especially if you have never met or spoken to them before.

● Have a clear speaking voice

Don't mumble on the 'phone or to customers. You should make eye contact if dealing directly with customers and speak clearly to avoid misunderstanding of messages.

● Be tactful

Even if you know the customer is wrong, be tactful and if necessary refer them to a senior staff member or your employer to deal with. *Never be rude to a customer* . . . no matter how you are provoked.

● Have a good level of English

You don't have to have an 'A' level in English, but it helps if you can spell and you know where to put an apostrophe S. It is not uncommon to find your employer can't spell—he runs a company and is successful. He will be employing you to type up his correspondence and see to mundane things such as correct grammar on letters!

If your spelling isn't up to scratch, you can always invest in a good dictionary or enrol at an evening class to brush up.

● Be numerate

You don't have to know how to work out the area of a field if $A = X$ and $B = Z$. However, you should be able to add, subtract, divide and multiply, with or without the aid of a calculator. You should also be able to transfer figures from calculator to paper and *always* double-check your figures for accuracy.

● Use your initiative and common sense

You should be able to work on your own and use your initiative for simple problems which happen throughout the day. Suppose you've run out of milk—you know the boss has visitors arriving in half an hour. Go and get some more milk! Don't wait to be told!

Management decisions should still be passed through your employer, eg a salesman has arrived with brochures for new office furniture. It is not up to you to order yourself a new crushed velvet office chair—this is a decision you leave to your employer.

● Respect confidentiality

It is important not to gossip about your employer or the people you work with. If someone shares a confidence with you, don't spread it around the rest of the office or at the local pub in the evening. People will soon learn whether they can trust you or not.

● Be self-motivated

If you have run out of work don't sit and gaze around an untidy office. The time you have spare could be used in clearing up or sorting through old files. If you have a cleaner she/he will probably empty bins and vacuum floors. However, in smaller offices without a cleaner, someone has to do the job. During those quiet spells (if you have them) take time to clear up.

● Honesty—security of money

If you deal with petty cash, make sure the cash tin is not left around for anyone to help themselves to money. Regularly double-check the amount in the tin ties in with the amount in your petty cash book. Don't 'borrow' from the petty cash. This is a bad habit and one you should not get into.

- **Have a smart appearance and pay attention to cleanliness**

You should always be smart and pay attention to personal hygiene. There is nothing worse than working in an office with someone who is slovenly and has not bothered to wash before coming to work. If you work with someone who has a personal freshness problem, it is better to leave a more experienced member of staff to deal with it. Mishandled, this touchy subject could cause extreme embarrassment for both yourself and the person with the problem. And make sure you're not the person with the problem!

- **Be aware of health and safety at work**

Offices should practise the Health and Safety at Work Regulations. You should always be aware of them yourself and safe practices such as no trailing leads on typewriters and kettles, should be strictly adhered to. The Health and Safety Executive supply posters which should be displayed for all staff to read. Fire extinguishers should be present and checked regularly. Ensure fire exits are not blocked by boxes or filing cabinets.

The above should be a guide as to what personal qualities you should cultivate in yourself, if you don't already possess them. You will be learning all the time. Resist the temptation to pick up bad habits from 'old timers' who want to show you the ropes and teach you the tricks of the trade, especially if you know that their practices go against everything you have learned.

HEALTH AND SAFETY AT WORK QUIZ

Because HASAW (Health and Safety at Work) regulations are so important, they will be referred to throughout this book. Your awareness of dangers in an office situation starts here . . . look at the picture in fig. 2 and circle as many Health and Safety at Work risks you can find, and which you think could cause accidents in an office. See fig. 3 to check out how well you did:

- Did you find all of them?

- Are you aware of why they are risks?

Look around your own home and see if there is anything you believe may lead to an accident. Examples of dangerous practices can range from badly stacked books teetering on the edge of your bookcase,

Fig. 2. Health and safety at work—how many risks can you spot?

just waiting to fall off, to a boiling saucepan on the cooker whose handle is sticking out ready for you to walk into.

Think safety—accidents can and will happen but don't be the cause of them.

CASE STUDIES

To help set the scene, we will introduce you to three people in the form of case studies. We will follow their progress throughout the subsequent chapters.

Lee

Lee's parents both work in offices and their son is keen to follow suit—good money, working indoors—it definitely appeals to him.

Lee is sixteen and still at school. He has passed his RSA I Typewriting Skills and Word Processing. His hobbies include football and playing computer games, both of which take up a great deal of his spare time

Chriss

Chriss is twenty-nine, a single parent, and her youngest of two children starts school next month. She hasn't worked for eight years but has been attending night school to brush up on her typing. She

Fig. 3. Health and safety at work—the hazards are circled. Can you spot any more?

had attained an RSA II Typewriting Skills whilst still at school. She is currently taking a course in word processing.

Jackie

Jackie lives with her mother as her parents are divorced. Her mother is unemployed and has a bit of a drink problem. Jackie has a Saturday job, working in the local shop to make a bit of money to help her mother out.

Jackie, sixteen, is struggling at school—her spelling isn't good, but she is trying hard. She finally achieves a pass in RSA CLAIT (Computer Literacy and Information Technology) and an RSA I in Word Processing.

SUMMARY

Here are the personal qualities you need to work in an office. How would you rate yourself on each? Score 3 for excellent, 2 for good, 1 for fair, 0 for weak.

- Be reliable   _____

- Have confidence—know your business   _____

- Be helpful   _____
- Be cheerful and friendly   _____
- Have a clear speaking voice   _____
- Be tactful   _____
- Have a good level of English   _____
- Be numerate   _____
- Use your initiate and common sense   _____
- Respect confidentiality   _____
- Be self-motivated   _____
- Honesty—security of money   _____
- Have a smart appearance, pay attention to
  cleanliness   _____
- Awareness of Health and Safety at Work   _____

Personal Qualities Score Rating

42–35   Very good—no doubt you'll be an asset to any employer—but don't let it go to your head.

35–21   Good—you could make a good office worker. Continue to cultivate your personal qualities and you'll go far.

21–7   A few loose ends, but if your self-motivation is high you could make it in an office. Good luck.

7–0   Do you really think office work is for you? If so, you will need to look closely at improving your personal qualities. You've made a start by reading this book.

DISCUSSION POINTS

1   Do you think you have the right personality and attitude to work closely with others in an office situation? What do you consider to be your best personal quality?

2   A lot of young people want to 'work with computers'. Unless you have specific training (*not* basic computer literacy or an avid interest in computer games) it is unlikely you will be offered a position solely working with computers, unless it is as a word processing/dataprocessing operator. How flexible are you willing to be in your choice of office career if you cannot get what you want immediately?

3   You are offered further training in office skills, all expenses paid by your company, which involves attending college one evening a week. You have to decide whether or not to accept the offer. What would your own decision be?

2
The Right Qualifications

ARE YOU QUALIFIED?

When you apply for an office position, you cannot prove to a prospective employer you are the right person for the job—although an interview is an excellent stage to put your case forward. But first, you have to get an interview!

Usually, you will receive an application form, which should be filled in and returned with a Curriculum Vitae (a document giving details of previous work experience and school qualifications). Unfortunately, neither of these documents will encourage an employer to call you for interview unless they know you, or there is something which indicates you can do the job.

Showing you have some office skills qualifications or have previous experience in office work may help you get the interview. It is a fact that employers often receive dozens of applicants for one job—most application forms end in the bin. Fig. 4 shows a typical advertisement for an office vacancy.

OFFICE JUNIOR REQUIRED

For busy doctor's surgery. Experience not essential but good typing skills are (RSA I or equivalent)

35 hours per week Mon—Fri

Apply in writing only with CV to:

Miss B Chinn, Practice Manager, Grove Road, Portsmouth

Closing date: 11 December 19—

Fig. 4. Advertisement for office vacancy.

What qualifications do you need?

Both RSA and Pitman Examination Institutes offer a variety of qualifications. As the qualification lists for both examination boards are similar, I shall concentrate on just one—the RSA.

Basic qualification requirements in an office are keyboarding skills. If you possess the following, it may help you to get your foot in the door:

Single subjects

RSA I	Typewriting Skills
RSA I	Word Processing

Other qualifications could include

RSA I	Data processing
RSA I	Spreadsheet
RSA II	Typewriting Skills
RSA II	Word Processing

There are many other qualifications available and lists of these can be obtained from schools, colleges and YT (youth training) schemes on request, but the above are the most widely recognised by employers.

If you are at college or on a youth training scheme you can obtain additional 'vocational' qualifications. You need work experience to complete these (vocational = pertaining to a trade or occupation or in preparation for a trade or occupation). The qualification takes the form of a diary, which you complete to show a written record of achievement. The evidence in your record book has to be signed by your work placement supervisor/trainer when they believe you are competent.

NVQs (National Vocational Qualifications) are offered by most examination boards, including RSA, Pitman and City and Guilds. Again, details of these and other NVQs can be obtained from colleges and youth training schemes. Four of the qualifications are named below *(NVQ Qualifications in Business Administration)*:

Business Administration	Level 1
Business Administration (Administrative)	Level 2
Business Administration (Financial)	Level 2
Business Administration (Secretarial)	Level 2

HOW AND WHERE TO QUALIFY

Depending on your age and personal situation there are several ways to get suitable office skills qualifications.

Qualifying at school
14–16 year age group—not all schools offer keyboarding skills, but many do. If you think you would like to work in an office and are about to choose your options, discuss this with your teacher.

Your school will supply the resources you need and usually pay for any examinations you take. They will also arrange for two weeks work experience with a local employer during your last year.

Qualifying at college
16+ age group—Colleges have specialised courses in business administration and offer a variety of subjects, including keyboarding. Depending on your age and circumstances, you could gain a place at college and take the qualifications you need.

Most colleges start their yearly term in September and as part of the course, arrange a two-week (possibly longer) 'taster' in office work by placing you with an employer. Check out your local college for commencement dates and length of courses.

Your tuition and resources are usually covered by the college if you have recently left school and join a full-time course. If you are a more 'mature'student you may have to pay for your own course. You may also have to pay for part-time courses. In certain circumstances, you may be able to obtain financial assistance—contact your local college for details of whether or not you are eligible.

Youth Training
16-18 age group—Youth training schemes also have specialised NVQ courses in business administration, and incorporate keyboarding skills as part of their curriculum.

They will find you a sponsor (usually a company local to your scheme) who will give you the opportunity to train in their office. You will be expected to return to the YT scheme or to a local college for training towards your qualifications, either once a week or on a 'block' basis for a week at a time.

You will be paid a training allowance of £29.50 (16-17 years) or £35.00 (17 years and over). Some schemes also pay travel expenses if it costs you more than £3.00 per week to get to your placement.

Many sponsors pay trainees in addition to the above if their work is good, and often offer a full-time position at the end of the training course.

Employment training
This is similar to youth training, but is aimed at the over-18 age group. There are several government-run training courses for adults, and full details can be obtained at your local Jobcentre.

Evening classes

Local schools and colleges usually run evening classes for people who work full-time or cannot study during the day. Most keyboarding skills can be learned here, although not all offer NVQs. They may offer specialised courses in bookkeeping. Again, check out your local school or college for details.

The cost of these courses will vary, and you will be expected to pay for your tuition, resources and examinations except in special circumstances. You may also get a reduction in your fee if you are unemployed. They do not offer work experience.

Private colleges and training agencies

There are many private colleges or training agencies who supply private training. For a list of these in your area, look under 'Secretarial Training' in your *Yellow Pages*. As some of these are fairly expensive, it is best to check out fees before enrolling and ensure they offer the qualifications you specifically require.

They usually offer a variety of business administration courses and keyboarding skills. You will be expected to pay for your tuition, resources and examiniations. They do not generally offer work experience.

Home study

You will have to be very self-motivated for home study, and push yourself on to complete the course. If you put off the inevitable work to watch your favourite TV programme, or continually make excuses to start, you may find this course is not for you and you will have wasted your money.

If you are self-motivated, and feel you would like to give it a try, colleges and private training organisations may be able to supply home study material. You can also find home study courses advertised in newspapers . . . but take care to chose one that has been personally recommended by someone you know, or is a well-established organisation known by you in your area.

They offer a variety of business administration and keyboarding skills courses. You will be expected to pay for your tuition, resources and examinations . They do not offer work experience.

You will have to deliver, or send by post, your work to be marked, which should be returned as soon as you have completed the assignments.

DO YOU NEED WORK EXPERIENCE?

The answer to that question, is no, but it helps if you do have some experience.

Most offices are very busy and do not always have time to spend 'showing you the ropes' on your first day. If you know how to photocopy or answer the telephone it is a definite advantage. However, it isn't essential.

If you work in a small office and can use your initiative, watch and learn from your employer or other staff as they answer the 'phone and file documents. Don't sit and daydream . . . especially if you are being paid.

Where can you get work experience?
Your final year at school
If you are at school, you may be offered two weeks work experience during your final year. Use the two weeks wisely. Don't use it as an excuse to have two weeks away from school and think it is a good skive, but learn as much as you can. If you've made a good impression, who knows, you may be offered a job when you leave school. If not, ask if they will give you a reference when you do apply for a job.

College placements
The same applies to work experience at college. Colleges arrange placements to give you a real feel or taste of office work. Help where you can in your office placement and don't sit around reading a magazine or gazing into outer space. As with work experience at school, you may be able to use the placement as a reference when you leave college, or be offered a job when you have completed the course.

Youth training
Youth training courses offer you a work placement. It takes at least a month to settle in and you should stick to it and give it a real go. You cannot possibly know whether or not you will like the job in less time than that. If it doesn't work out, you may be offered another placement . . . or, if you aren't really suited to office work, be transferred to another training area, such as retail. You will gain something from every job you do, even if it is only how to fix the photocopier when it jams!

Using friends and contacts
Do you know a member or friend of the family who runs an office and is desperate for some help? Offer your services, even if you do it for nothing. Take advantage of the situation if your offer is accepted and learn as much as you can. Who knows, you may even get paid, or even better be offered a proper job at the end of it.

Other local opportunities
Other part-time work, such as working in a local shop, is also good work experience. You may not have to type or use a word processor, but you may be involved in dealing with the public, answering the 'phone, stock control, handling money and credit cards, filing invoices, credit notes and delivery notes, all of which can be transferred to the office.

In conclusion if you want to get qualifications and work experience, it's up to you to make the effort yourself.

CASE STUDIES

Your personal circumstance is a great motivator and as our case studies continue, a picture will form of how our backgrounds affect the way we act. Being male or female makes very little difference these days where work opportunities in an office are concerned, but your personal motivation does.

Lee
Lee has an allowance of £20 a week from his parents. He is offered the chance to work on a Saturday morning for his father in the office.

'How much will you pay me?' Lee asks.

'There' s no money involved, Lee, but I thought it would be good experience for you.'

'It's not worth giving up my Saturday if you're not paying me. Besides I promised my mate I'd go to the match with him.' Pausing for thought, Lee adds. 'I suppose it would be good experience, though. If the team's playing away next week, I'll come in then.'

Chriss
Chriss has asked a woodworm specialist to give her a quotation. She has found woodworm holes in her loft, and is concerned it will spread.

'Won't be able to get the quote to you for a couple of weeks, I'm afraid. I used to have a lady who typed them up for me at home, but she moved away.'

Chriss is desperate to make some extra money. 'I'll do it for you,' she says, immediately. 'I've got a typewriter. I'll do the first one for free so you can see my work. If you're happy, perhaps we could discuss a fee.'

The woodworm specialist is a little stunned by her enthusiasm, but decides to give Chriss a try.

Jackie

Jackie works at the local shop on Saturdays. She needs the job as her mother is unemployed and money is tight. As well as stacking shelves and dealing with customers, she handles cash and credit cards, counts the stock and reorders when items run low. Although at first nervous, she is used to the customers now, and tries to be helpful and cheerful.

During school holidays she sometimes helps out during the week. She checks stock against delivery notes and files paperwork when deliveries come in. She also answers the telephone if her supervisor is busy.

SUMMARY

Below is a checklist of where qualifications and work experience can be obtained. The list is not exhaustive and you should keep your eyes and ears alert to opportunities to gain work experience.

	Qualification	Work Experience
School	☑	☑
College	☑	☑
Youth training	☑	☑
Employment training	☑	☑
Evening classes	☑	☒
Private colleges and training agencies	☑	☒
Home study	☑	☒
Part-time work in retail	☒	☑

√ indicates that work experience is offered.

× indicates that it is not usual to offer work experience.

DISCUSSION POINTS

1 Have you given any thought to the future training and qualifications you would like to gain? What would you like to achieve within the next two years?

2 If you are still at school or college, can you think of any way you could personally gain work experience? Have you thought of asking family or friends if they need help at work?

You are offered work experience at the weekend. Are you willing to give up some of your time to work, paid or unpaid? If you aren't, give a valid reason for your decision.

3 If a number of years have passed since you last worked, some of
   your skills may be outdated—he world of work is changing daily.
   List three procedures which have changed since you last
   worked.

Note: There are many office procedures books available which can
help you to update your skills—a list can be found at the back of this
book. If money is tight, visit your library and check out some of the
practical office procedures books available in the business section.

How to Know Your Rights at Work

Robert Spicer

A Practical Guide to Employment Law

'Clearly written in language readily understood by the layman . . . The text has
been well laid out and sections are clearly signposted . . . The extensive use of case
study materials is interesting and helpful . . . The book is not only relevant to
Careers Officers and their clients, but also to other people working in the employ-
ment/employment advisory field . . . The sort of book that can be easily dipped into
for specific information, but which is interesting enough in its own right to be read
from cover to cover.' *Careers Officer Journal.* 'Sets out in simple English everything
an employee can expect in today's working environment.' *Kent Evening Post.* Robert
Spicer MA (Cantab) is a practising barrister, legal editor and author who specialises
in employment law.

£6.99, 141pp illus. 1 85703 009 5.

Please add postage and packing (UK £1.00 per copy. Europe £2.00 per copy.
World £3.00 per copy airmail).

How To Books Ltd, Plymbridge House, Estover Road, Plymouth PL6 7PZ,
United Kingdom, Tel: (0752) 695745. Fax: 695699. Telex: 45635.

3
Getting Your First Office Job

PRODUCING A CURRICULUM VITAE

Before applying for jobs you should already have prepared a **curriculum vitae** (CV). A CV gives details of your past schooling, experience, employment and qualifications and should be prepared with a great deal of thought. The example in fig. 5 gives you an idea of a suitable layout of a CV and the sort of information a prospective employer may find of use when deciding whether or not it is worth interviewing you.

How to fill in your CV
Name, Address, Telephone Number, Date of Birth, Nationality and National Insurance Number
Fill in your own details plus your date of birth rather than your age (in case you have a birthday before you get to use your CV!).

Driving Licence
Some jobs involve driving (taking money to the bank, delivering or collecting goods) and a prospective employer may need to know whether you have a full or provisional licence and whether you have any convictions (his insurance may not cover staff with convictions on his policy if using a firm's vehicle). Be honest—he may ask you to produce your licence!

Education
Start with your most recent education. For example if you have just left school, been to college or on a training course, give details of this first. Put the dates you attended. If you cannot remember exactly, the month and year will be sufficient.

Qualifications
List any qualifications you have. Also include any examinations you have taken and are awaiting the results of, and any examinations you will be taking in the near future.

CURRICULUM VITAE

NAME:

ADDRESS:

TELEPHONE NUMBER:

DATE OF BIRTH:

NATIONALITY:

NATIONAL INSURANCE NO:

DRIVING LICENCE:

EDUCATION:

QUALIFICATIONS:

WORK EXPERIENCE:

HOBBIES:

OTHER INTERESTS:

REFERENCES:

Fig. 5. Typical layout of a curriculum vitae (CV).

Hobbies

List hobbies you really partake in. Don't write that you like to scuba dive if you can't even swim. BE TRUTHFUL. Your prospective employer may be able to scuba dive and ask questions you don't know the answers to. If you have lied and get the job, you will be found out in time.

Don't put down in your Hobby section that you like night-clubbing and dancing. This will probably give a prospective employer the idea that you may come into work with a hangover after a heavy weekend of getting on down at the local disco. Most people have a social life—it should be kept as part of your private life and is not really appropriate for entry on your CV. A future employer is more interested in such signs as whether you have shown initiative, learned any new skills, shown responsibility or a sense of community, and so on.

Other interests

This section is for activities you do not take part in regularly but feel it appropriate to add, for instance charity work or helping others. Again be honest here. It will help an employer to see what sort of person you are. If you have no other interests, however, leave out this heading.

Giving references

When choosing referees, you should ask the person first if they mind giving you a reference. The referees should be people who know you in a professional situation, such as teachers or previous employers. Your best friend or mother are not appropriate to give references as they are probably biased!

Where to get your CV typed to a professional standard

If you are applying for an office position, a nicely typed CV will be a way of showing your typing ability. Do you already have access to a typewriter or word processor? If not, ask friends or family if they will type your CV for you or allow you to use their equipment. Often, they will do this without expecting any payment.

If you are at school, college or on a YT scheme, your tutors will help you prepare and produce a CV.

If you are not able to draw on your friends or relations and have no access to equipment, there are secretarial agencies who will write and type a CV for you to a professional standard. However, they do make a charge for this service, the cost of which varies, so be prepared to part with some cash!

CURRICULUM VITAE

NAME:	Kellie Henry
ADDRESS:	1 Wilmir, Twynhams Hill, Waltham Heath, SOUTHAMPTON SO3 2NG
TELEPHONE NUMBER:	0329 896170
DATE OF BIRTH:	14 January 1976
NATIONALITY:	British
NATIONAL INSURANCE NO:	YL 458956
DRIVING LICENCE:	Full/Clean
EDUCATION:	Swanmore County Secondary, Swanmore, Southampton 1988–1993

QUALIFICATIONS:

GCSE
English Lit/Lang	Grade C
Maths	Grade D
Geography	Grade G
History	Grade F
Science	Grade F

QUALIFICATIONS:

RSA I
C.L.A.I.T.	Stage I
Word Processing	Stage I
Typewriting Skills	Stage I

First Aid Certificate (Red Cross)

WORK EXPERIENCE:

1993–present: Part-time weekend employment at local garage. Duties included serving customers, handling cash, cheques and credit cards, restocking shelves and clearing up.

1993: 2 weeks work experience at Cobalt Printers. Duties included answering the telephone, filing, photocopying and typing envelopes.

HOBBIES:

Reading

OTHER INTERESTS:

Once a year I help to raise funds for the local disabled association by walking for charity.

REFERENCES

Mrs Green, Cobalt Printers, Forest Lane, Southampton. Tel: 0703 892860

Mr Stubbs, Swanmore Secondary School, Swanmore, Southampton Tel: 0489 764230

Fig. 6. Completed curriculum vitae.

WHERE TO LOOK FOR A JOB

Once you have gained the appropriate qualifications/experience there are several ways to search for your first job.

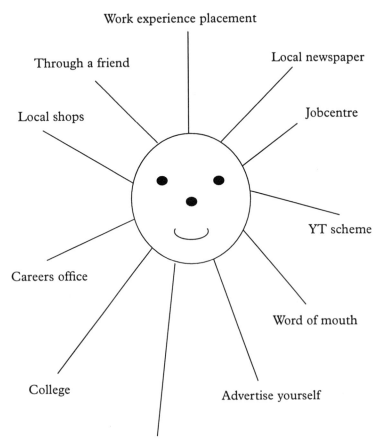

Work experience placement

Contact your previous work experience placement. Ask if they know of anyone looking for some help in their office. If they do and remember you as a good worker they will be happy to recommend you to another employer. (However, if you were lazy and showed little initiative they will not risk recommending you to anyone.) If they have an opening themselves, they may offer you the job!

Through a friend/family member

Ask friends who are working if they know of any jobs being advertised or vacant at their place of work. Again they will probably only give you a positive answer if they know you will work—their personal reputation will be at stake if you turn out to be a poor worker.

Local newspapers

Local newspapers usually have a specific evening to advertise for jobs, usually Thursday, although they may still have a few vacancies advertised on other evenings.

Look for appropriate situations and contact the advertisers straight away. If the advertisement asks for a written application DO NOT TELEPHONE. Send CVs with application unless otherwise stated.

Local shops

Some vacancies are advertised in local shop windows or notice-boards. Quite often these will include a telephone number for you to call. Contact them straight away—the vacancy may already have been filled and you don't want to waste time on something that has already gone.

Jobcentres

Competition at jobcentres is high. Pop in every day if you can, as vacancies are coming in all the time. If you live several miles from the Centre, this may not be practical.

Careers offices

The Careers Service also have vacancies. Again, it is a matter of calling in each day in case a new job is being advertised.

Youth training schemes

Youth training schemes usually find jobs for their trainees and match the person to the position.

If you find a job yourself, perhaps through a friend, or a friend of a friend, and want to gain more qualifications you can approach a YT scheme, who will take you on and pay a contribution towards your wages.

Colleges
College notice boards advertise job vacancies.

Word of mouth
You may hear of a vacancy through conversation with others. Follow up any leads but don't be too pushy. Someone else may already be in mind for the job.

Staff notice boards
Again, friends and acquaintances come in handy here—ask if they mind checking their Staff Notice Board for any vacancy that may be available. But don't become a pain by harassing people.

Advertise yourself
Write to companies asking if they have any vacancies at present or if they will keep you in mind for the future. Look up names of prospective employers in the 'phone book. These can be small or large companies in your area—companies you wouldn't mind working for and who are within travelling distance from your home. Enclose a CV when you write.

You may write forty letters and this will cost you time, postage and stationery—but it may get you a job! Always enclose a stamped addressed envelope. An employer is more likely to reply (even if it is to return your letter with a short note to say 'no') given an SAE.

Who to write to
You should address your application to the Personnel Department. If you know the name of a contact in the company, for example, the director or personnel manager, write directly to them.

What to say
In fig. 7, an example has been laid out to show you the sort of information which should be included if you intend to mail shot prospective employers.

HOW TO WRITE AN APPLICATION LETTER

When a job is advertised, it may ask you to telephone for an application form or write a letter of application.

1 Wilmir
Twynhams Hill
Waltham Heath
SOUTHAMPTON SO3 2NG

8 November 19—

The Personnel Manager
Fareport Electrics
Mill Lane
FAREHAM   PO12 4QG

Dear Sirs

I am currently seeking employment in office skills and wonder if your company has any openings. If you have nothing at present, I would be pleased if you would keep my details on file should anything become available in the future.

I have experience in office work and also several keyboarding qualifications (see enclosed CV). I would be happy to attend an interview at short notice.

I look forward to hearing from you and enclose a stamped addressed envelope for your reply.

Yours faithfully

Kellie Henry (Miss)

Enc

Fig. 7. Sample letter—how to sell yourself.

- If a telephone call is requested, and you don't like making phone calls—don't panic. You will probably only be asked for your name and address so that an application form can be sent to you. It is unlikely the employer will give you the third degree over the phone.

- If the advertisement states: 'Please write for an application form,' your letter should be short and to the point, neatly handwritten or typed (fig. 8).

- If the advertisement states: 'Please send CV and details of previous work experience,' the letter should be written with a few details about your work experience and examinations, but the main information should be contained in your enclosed CV. Again, it can either be neatly handwritten or typed (fig. 9).

1 Wilmir
Twynhams Hill
Waltham Heath
SOUTHAMPTON SO3 2NG

9 November 19—

The Personnel Manager
Fareport Electrics
Mill Lane
FAREHAM   PO12 4QG

Dear Sirs

RE: OFFICE JUNIOR POSITION

The above was advertised in last night's Evening Echo and I would like to apply for the position.

Would you kindly forward an application form to me as soon as possible. I look forward to hearing from you.

Yours faithfully

Kellie Henry (Miss)

Fig. 8. Application letter (one).

1 Wilmir
Twynhams Hill
Waltham Heath
SOUTHAMPTON SO3 2NG

9 November 19—

The Personnel Manager
Fareport Electrics
Mill Lane
FAREHAM   PO12 4QG

Dear Sirs

RE: OFFICE JUNIOR POSITION

The above post was advertised in last night's Evening Echo and I would like to apply for the position.

I have some work experience and spent two weeks at Cobalt Printers last year, working in their office—they will be happy to supply a reference.

I have passed several examinations and will be taking my RSA II Typewriting in January. I enclose full details on my CV. If you require further information please do not hesitate to contact me.

I am available for interview at short notice and look forward to hearing from you in the near future should you wish to consider my application.

Yours faithfully

Kellie Henry (Miss)

Enc

Fig. 9. Application letter (two).

YOU'VE GOT AN INTERVIEW—WHAT NEXT?

When you receive a letter asking you to attend an interview, you should reply straight away to confirm the date. You should also congratulate yourself—you obviously have something that the employer is interested in. Now it's up to you to make the most of the opportunity to impress them!

Write to confirm the interview

It is important to write to confirm you will be attending the interview. You would be surprised how many young people don't do this— and even more surprised at the number who don't bother to turn up for the interview at all! With a little bit of thought, you can impress a prospective employer without even trying. Remember employers are human too, and they do notice common courtesy.

When you write the letter, keep it business-like. The two letters in figs. 10 and 11, are from Kellie Henry and, again, they are comparisons of 'how to' and 'how not to' write. I leave it to you to choose which letter is the most professional, and which you think would impress a prospective employer.

If you chose the letter in fig. 10 you are on the right lines. However, if you chose the letter in fig. 11 you will not impress anyone. It's far too familiar and very unprofessional. You don't want to put the employer off before you've arrived at the interview room.

Be prepared for the interview

Remember you are now about to 'sell' yourself, and must look on the interview as your finest performance. You have to prepare yourself well beforehand—competition for the job will be steep and if you don't make a special effort, others will.

There are several books, videos and television programmes geared specifically towards helping you succeed at an interview. You may already have had some training in interview techniques at school, college or on YT, but it won't hurt to brush up before you embark on a real interview. *How to Pass that Interview* by Judith Johnstone is an excellent book, which will give you all the help you need.

Before the interview

Check things out before the interview—never leave anything to the last minute:

Check out the job details
Check out the job description and company details. You may have

1 Wilmir
Twynhams Hill
Waltham Heath
SOUTHAMPTON SO3 2NG

20 November 19—

Mr Reeve
The Personnel Manager
Fareport Electrics
Mill Lane
FAREHAM   PO12 4QG

Dear Mr Reeve

RE: OFFICE JUNIOR POSITION

Thank you for your letter of 19 November offering me an interview for Thursday, 25 November at 2.00 pm.

I will be pleased to attend the interview and look forward to meeting you next week.

Yours sincerely

Kellie Henry (Miss)

Fig. 10. Confirmation letter (one).

1 Wilmir
Twynhams Hill
Waltham Heath
SOUTHAMPTON SO3 2NG

20 November 19—

Mr Reeve
The Personnel Manager
Fareport Electrics
Mill Lane
FAREHAM   PO12 4QG

Dear Mr Reeve

RE: OFFICE JUNIOR POSITION

Thank you for your letter of 19 November offering me an interview for Thursday, 25 November at 2.00 pm.

I was really chuffed when I received your letter—I never thought I'd ever get an interview because I've been trying for about three months now.

I can't wait to meet you next week, and I'm sure you will be impressed with me as I am a good office worker. See you next week.

Yours sincerely

Kellie Henry (Miss)

Fig. 11. Confirmation letter (two).

received information about the company—make sure you read it and understand a bit about the company and what your role would be.

Find out what you can from other sources about the company—from people who work there, from Careers or the Jobcentre. It will give you good background information and help you to prepare questions to be used at the end of the interview.

Be clear about your reasons

Check out why you want the job. You will more than likely be asked why you applied to work for this particular company. If you look blank and have no idea how to answer the question, your interviewer may think you *don't* want the job.

Be ready for the questions

What questions will you ask at your interview? A prospective employer is almost sure to ask if there is anything you would like to know. If you sit in dumb silence, shaking your head in bewilderment, he will realise you haven't given much thought to the interview. But don't invent a few questions off the top of your head if they have no relevance to the job just for the sake of it. If all the questions you planned to ask have already been answered, then say so.

Check your appearance

Check out the clothes you are going to wear. Although this may seem fairly basic, it is better to try on several different outfits the day before, than leave it until an hour before you are due to leave for the interview.

You want to be as calm as possible on the day—the stress of deciding which clothes may or may not give the right impression, should take place before that!—especially if you find your skirt seam has split and needs repair, or your best shirt has a chocolate stain on the front.

Check out your shoes. If you haven't cleaned them for a while, and usually only wipe them over with a dishcloth, give them a real treat of polish and a good brush up. Quite often people arrive for an interview, their hair beautifully styled, their clothes immaculate, but with their shoes scuffed and dirty.

Don't think an employer won't notice—he will! He may also see the lack of polish as a reflection of your attitude to work . . . (Can't be bothered to finish off the job properly?') Dirty shoes could lose you the interview.

Check out your appearance. Don't go over the top with make-up or extravagant hair-styles. Hair, beards and moustaches should be trimmed and neat. If you wear glasses, are they clean and in good repair? Ask for others' opinion if you're not sure if you look OK . . . and make sure it's someone prepared to give you an honest opinion.

How will you get there in time?
Check out bus/train times, car parking, etc, and how long it will take you to get to the place of interview. Find out exactly where the work place is by travelling there before the interview—perhaps a family member or friend will take you there if you don't have your own transport. Do not arrive late at the interview, unless you have an extremely good reason for it.

What will you need to take?
Check out things to take with you. Take the letter inviting you to interview. It will have the address and telephone number of the company . . . just in case you need them. Take a list of questions you have prepared (although you shouldn't read these off the sheet at your interview). Take examination certificates and evidence of work experience.

Take a bottle of Tippex and a typing eraser. If you are given a typing test and don't know how to use the correcting key, you will feel better with something to help you out. Interviews make people nervous, and a typing test can be difficult. Don't be embarrassed if you do make mistakes—interviewers will know the pressure you are under.

Take a handkerchief—especially if you suffer with hay fever or have an allergy. Even if you don't, it always pays to be prepared for any emergency.

Personal hygiene
Check out your personal hygiene. Bathe or shower, wash your hair and clean your teeth on the day. All are basic rules of hygiene and should not only be a priority for the interview, but also for the rest of your working life. Offices are often warm, and you may perspire more than usual at an interview, so make sure you use a deodorant.

Take a look at your hands. Do you have paint or grease on them? Are your nails clean and tidy. If not, do something about it.

Use the pre-interview checklist to help you

1   Check out the job description and company details.   ☐

2   Check out questions you will ask at the interview.   ☐

3   Check out why you want the job.   ☐

4   Check out the clothes you are going to wear.   ☐

5   Check out your shoes.   ☐

6   Check out your appearance.   ☐

7   Check out bus/train times, car parking, etc.   ☐

8   Check out things to take with you.   ☐

9   Check out your personal hygiene.   ☐

The night before

Make sure you have everything you need for the following day and your clothes are clean and ironed. Lay them out together with your cleaned shoes. Read through your list of questions and answers prepared beforehand, just to refresh your memory.

Avoid going out for a drink with your friends, who want to wish you good luck. You may end up drinking more than you'd planned, which could be a bigger headache than you ever imagined . . . if you wake up with a hangover, your performance at your interview will suffer.

Have an early night and don't forget to set your alarm if your interview is first thing in the morning!

INTERVIEW DAY

Time to go to the interview

Have a light breakfast, or lunch if the interview is in the afternoon. Avoid garlic and spicy foods—you don't want to put the interviewer off by breathing toxic fumes into his face . . . and you don't want an upset stomach.

Reread your letter before you leave, just in case there is something you missed when you first received your invitation to the interview. Check out the interview time again, and see that your watch is accurate. Collect all the paperwork prepared the day before and aim to arrive at least fifteen minutes before the interview.

If you are *unavoidably* delayed, contact the employer by 'phone if possible and explain briefly the problem. Perhaps they will put the interview forward, or call you in another day. If you cannot contact them immediately, get to the interview as soon as you can and apologise. If you have missed your interview, they may decide to give you another. If they do, make sure you arrive on time or they will probably think you don't really want the job.

If you are ill, again contact them by 'phone and explain briefly the problem. Ask them if it is possible to arrange another interview date.

Hopefully, neither of the above events will happen, and you will arrive at the interview venue in plenty of time, unflustered and quietly confident.

The waiting game

While you wait for your interview, ask where the cloakroom is so you can check your appearance, visit the toilet and wash your hands. If you meet any of the staff during your wait, be polite and friendly. You won't know who they are, but they will know you are being interviewed with a view to joining their staff team. In other words, they will be checking out applicants, and may have a say in who they work with.

Read through your notes again if necessary, and try to relax yourself by slow, deep breathing. Don't smoke or chew gum. These two will definitely put a black mark against your name. Even if you feel you need a cigarette, try to manage without. If the interviewer is a non-smoker, she/he is unlikely to appreciate the aroma of cigarette smoke, which will cling to your clothes. You may not smell it yourself, but she/he will.

If other candidates are in the waiting area with you, you may want to engage them in conversation, or you may wish to sit quietly and gather your thoughts. It's up to you to gauge the mood of the other candidates and yourself.

The interviewer summons you

'Miss Henry? Mr Reeve will see you now.' Smile as you are escorted towards your interviewer. Take a deep breath. The time has come to sell yourself and make a good impression. If there are several interviewers, acknowledge them all by smiling at them in turn.

Say hello and, if invited, shake hands with the interviewer. If there is more than one interviewer, try to remember their names. Only sit down on invitation and don't assume the only chair is for you.

If you have a bag or folder, place it on the floor by your chair. Try not to fidget, flick you hair or play with fluff balls on your jumper. Hold your hands loosely on your lap . . . and don't pick your nails.

During the interview

Speak clearly and maintain eye contact with the interviewer. He or she will try to relax you with a few initial questions—try to keep your answers direct and simple and don't waffle.

Take your interview seriously. Don't laugh or giggle, pull faces or make jokes. Don't lose concentration. If you do, the interviewer will think you've also lost interest.

Ask for clarification if you don't understand a question. Don't try to answer something you don't understand—you will look silly if you have got it completely wrong.

- Don't be offended if the interviewer asks questions about your family background. If you've never worked before and have no previous experience, the information may help to give a clearer picture of what you are capable of.

- Don't be negative or blame other people for short-comings in your life, or the fact you didn't get very good GCSE grades at school. Accept responsibility for yourself and be positive about your future and additional training you hope to get.

If you are asked to take a typing test, don't panic. Before you start, look at the typewriter and check to see if there is a lift-off tape, where the margin keys are, etc. If there is no automatic correcting mechanism, you have your bottle of Tippex to help you. Better still, don't make any mistakes!

Don't rush it, but don't take too much time either—you don't want the interviewer to think you'll take that long to type letters if you're offered the position. Take care to produce good, clean typing, properly laid out to RSA I standard, and ensure your Tippex is dry before retyping correct information. You don't want to leave a splodge of white on your prospective employers new electronic typewriter. Check carefully for errors before handing back work for examination.

At the end of the interview, ask any questions still unanswered. If, however, they have all been covered, say so.

In the closing stages, it is appropriate to ask when you can expect to hear the result of the interview. The interviewer is not there to make you suffer, and will be happy to give you an indication of how long the selection process will take.

Time to leave

It's almost over. You now have to leave the room and make way for the next applicant. Collect your bag, folder, etc, and shake hands with the interviewer if you think it appropriate. Smile and thank them for their time before exiting the room. Don't rush out, as though there were no tomorrow, but pause at the door, turn and thank them again . . . then close the door and breath a sigh of relief. The worst bit is over, now you have to wait for the result. Go home, and make yourself a cup of tea, cut a slice of cake, put your feet up and relax.

YOU'VE GOT THE JOB!

You may receive a telephone call to give you the good news (and sometimes this can be the same day as the interview) or you may receive a letter.

Don't be surprised if you are offered a trial period contract. The period could be from one to six months. This is fairly common practice these days, and gives both the employer and the employee time to decide whether:

(a) your work is up to scratch
(b) you fit in with the existing staff team.

If you irritate people, cause trouble between staff, your work is poor and you tend to be laid back and lazy, you may be asked to leave. Remember, although you have been given the opportunity to prove yourself, there are many unemployed people who would love the chance to step into your shoes if you don't make the effort.

Write to accept the position

Whichever method the employer chooses to inform you of your success, if you decide to accept the position, it is important to acknowledge this by letter. The letter should be business-like and to the point. Fig. 12 shows one way to write an acceptance letter.

CASE STUDIES

Lee

Lee has now worked in his father's office for a couple of Saturdays. He sees a vacancy in the Admin office on the Company notice board and decides to try for it. He visits the office and collects an application form.

Lee had seen a video on interview techniques on TV and knows how to handle himself at an interview. He impresses the recruitment officer with his enthusiasm and, after passing a word processing test, is offered the job on a three-month trial period.

1 Wilmir
Twynhams Hill
Waltham Heath
SOUTHAMPTON SO3 2NG

29 November 19—

Mr Reeve
The Personnel Manager
Fareport Electrics
Mill Lane
FAREHAM   PO12 4QG

Dear Mr Reeve

RE: OFFICE JUNIOR POSITION

Thank you very much for your letter offering me the above position.

I have read the Conditions of Employment and am happy to accept your offer. I will return the signed copy when I commence work on 8 December at 9.00 am.

I look forward to meeting you again and hope that I will become a valuable member of your staff team.

Yours sincerely

Kellie Henry (Miss)

Fig. 12. Job acceptance letter.

Chriss

A friend of the woodworm specialist is looking for an administrator for his office. He mentions this to Chriss and suggests she contact his friend, Mr Roberts.

Chriss telephones and an informal interview is arranged. She is keen to get the job, so finds out as much as she can about the company, mainly from the woodworm specialist. During the interview, Mr Roberts is impressed with the research Chriss has obviously done. He has also done some research of his own and has checked with his friend regarding the quality of Chriss's work.

Mr Roberts telephones the same evening and offers Chriss a full-time contract, subject to discussions re wages, hours and so on.

Jackie

On leaving school, the Career Service suggests that Jackie joins a YT scheme. They arrange an interview for her and she starts the next week.

After a month in-house, training towards qualifications and interview techniques, an interview is arranged for Jackie and another YT trainee. At the interview, Jackie doesn't understand some of the questions the recruitment officer asks her. Feeling inadequate, she begins to stare vacantly around the room. She believes she isn't good enough for the job. The other trainee is taken on—the recruitment officer felt Jackie wasn't interested in the job.

A few weeks later, Jackie is offered a second interview. She has talked to her tutor and has been given extra help on her interview techniques. The interview goes well, and she is offered a placement.

DISCUSSION POINTS

1   If you are actively seeking a job, you will have to attend an interview. Perhaps you live in jeans and sweatshirts. Do you have something to wear if you are called for an interview at short notice? If not, it would be wise to buy something, or to approach a friend or family member who will lend you something suitable if you cannot afford to buy your own at present.

2   Think of, and write down, five questions you would like to ask at interview. If you have no idea of the type of questions to ask, get hold of one of the self-help books (most are stocked at the local library)—a list can be found at the back of this book, or talk to your tutor, parent or career's adviser.

3   Do you have a CV? If not, can you arrange to produce one, or know of someone who can help you?

4
In at the Deep End

PREPARING FOR DAY ONE

Everyone feels a bit nervous before their first day at work, so it is wise to prepare yourself beforehand. Don't leave everything to the last minute . . . finishing homework on Sunday night is OK when you're at school . . . but this is work.

By organising simple things—how to get to work, what to take with you, etc—your first day will get off to a good start.

Travelling to work
You should know where your place of work is, but it's important you arrive on time.

- Will you be going by bus? Find out where the nearest bus stop to your office is and how long it will take you to walk there. It is better to arrive twenty minutes early than ten minutes late.

- Will you be driving or riding a motor cycle? If so, find out how long it takes to get to work and what facilities there are for parking. If you need to use a public car park, check you have the correct change for the meter. You may be able to obtain a quarterly/yearly ticket from the appropriate authority (details are usually on notice boards in the car park) if you become a regular user of this facility.

- If you ride a cycle, again, find out where you can park it . . . and don't forget your security lock/chain.

Take some change with you
As well as money for parking, you may need some change for food and drink if your company has a food/drinks machine. It's no use taking a five or ten pound note, hoping someone will be able to change it for you early in the morning. It's better to be prepared—

you will know roughly how much to take depending on your personal needs.

What to wear
Decide the night before what you are going to wear. Dress smartly and wear something you feel comfortable in. Remember you will be representing your company and certain types of clothing are not really suitable. Don't dress to shock.

- If you are a female, avoid low-cut blouses, too-short skirts or four-inch heels.

- If you are a male, avoid T-shirts with obscene logos, cut-off jeans and 18-inch Doc Martens.

Remember to clean your shoes. You want to make a good impression on your first day.

Do I take anything with me?
The answer to this has to be yes. The old scout motto should be applied here—'Be prepared'.

The sort of things you need to take with you are fairly basic. You may not need them, but take them anyway.

- You will more than likely be nervous and may make more mistakes than usual if you are asked to type a letter. Most companies now use electronic typewriters which have a lift-off tape—that is, a correcting ribbon which lifts off errors from the paper. But what happens if the correcting ribbon is missing or has run out?

  If there is no Tippex in the office, or the one in the drawer has dried up, correcting errors on your first day can be a nightmare! You may feel you have wasted your money if you don't use them, but . . .

- You may not drink tea or coffee, but if you do, take your own cup. Some offices have drinks machines which supply plastic cups, others make their own and have a selection of cups for staff use. However, once a staff member has 'adopted' their own cup, woe betide anyone else who uses it. If you take your own cup, you won't be stepping on anyone's toes. Again, you may not need it, but take one—just in case.

- Take a packed lunch, or money to buy something to eat if there is a canteen or shop within easy walking distance. You may not feel like eating anything before you leave for work, but by mid-day your stomach will be rumbling.

- Take something to read at lunch break as the time can drag, especially if you share a staff room. By hiding yourself behind a book, you can gradually get used to your colleagues—although resist the temptation to read magazines or books during quiet spells in the office.

Example

'Have you seen my cup?' Ann asked after searching the office for ten minutes.

'Do you mean this one?' you ask innocently.

Ann glares at you from across the room. You are drinking from the bone china cup she brought in from home. 'I'd appreciate it,' she said crossly, 'If you brought you own in. Now if you don't mind, I'll have it back.'

You don't even have time to finish your tea as she snatches it from your hand. You have definitely made an enemy over something as trivial as a cup . . . but life's like that, and you're learning fast.

Personal hygiene

Lack of personal hygiene is inexcusable in an office. Even with advertisements and media exposure, it is surprising how many people are not aware they have a personal freshness problem. Every-one perspires, and occasionally, you will be aware you are sweating more than usual, for instance, during hot weather. Centrally heated offices can also make you sweat more.

Body odour causes offence to others in the office, and is embar-rassing for the unfortunate staff member who has to deal with the offending person. There are very simple guidelines, which if carried out regularly, can eliminiate the need for a quiet word being whis-pered in your ear . . . 'B.O.'

The night before

Have a bath or shower the night before, or first thing in the morning. If you perspire a lot, you may have to bath or shower every day. Make allowance for this if you intend to bath/shower in the morning and set your alarm accordingly.

Is getting up in the mornings difficult for you? If so, have a bath the night before. Don't kid yourself you will have time if you are one of the 'just one more minute and I'll get up' brigade.   Good intentions are all well and good, but we are talking *reality* here!

How to avoid nasty niffs
Use a antiperspirant/deodorant for protection against nasty niffs. However, unless you wash first, using a deodorant is not a lot of use. If you are just trying to mask the smell, it won't work, but it will produce a sickly pong which will probably be twice as bad.

If you are at work and begin to perspire, chemists and shops sell excellent spray-on deodorants (mostly ozone friendly) which can be used to freshen yourself up.   It is advisable to change the brand of deodorant from time to time, as your body may develop a resistance to their powers . . . and you may develop a problem.

Nails
Chek your nails are clean. If you make a cup of tea for a visitor, and pass the drink and a plate of biscuits with hands sporting grubby fingernails, your visitor may suspect that your hygiene habits leave a lot to be desired.

If you bite your nails and pick at the quicks until they bleed, how about giving it up? Chemists usually sell bitter-tasting liquids which are painted onto your nails. The foul taste of these liquids will bring your attention immediately to the problem, and hopefully, help you to stop.

Hair care
You don't have to spend pounds on fancy haircuts, but you should make sure your hair is neat and tidy. Regularly washing is also important as dirty, greasy hair is rather off-putting.

If you suffer with dandruff, medicated shampoos can be purchased from many shops. If you finish the bottle and think it hasn't worked, try a different brand.

If you have a beard or moustache, keep it trimmed and neat. Scraggy beards show a lack of care over your appearance, as does an unshaved face, sporting a five o'clock shadow. If you are growing a beard, stubble is unavoidable, but give yourself time in the mornings if you wish to remain clean-shaven.

Halitosis
Halitosis (bad breath) can cause offence. It can be caused by smoking, over-indulgence with garlic, curry the night before, rotting teeth, or simply poor dental hygiene.

On a daily basis it is up to you to maintain a routine, and brush your teeth at least twice a day—morning and night. If you can afford it, mouthwashes are excellent for ridding your mouth of bad breath. If possible, you should brush after every meal, but, realistically, it is unlikely to get done at work. Use dental floss (waxed or unwaxed 'cotton'). At first, you may not like the feel of using floss, but it is excellent for removing particles of rotting food which would otherwise sit and decay between your teeth.

If you chew breath-freshening gum, chew it and ditch it—chewing gum continually doesn't look good. Never talk to clients or answer the telephone with gum in your mouth.

Get yourself regular dental check-ups, once every six months: these are free if you are at school, full-time college, unemployed or pregnant. If none of these apply, costs vary depending on your dentist, but he/she should be able to give you a price for treatment before it is started.

Clean clothes

There is no point in bathing or showering if your clothes smell. Suits and jackets don't need cleaning too often, but you should keep a check on their freshness. Shirts and blouses, jumpers and tops, should be washed regularly.

If you perspire a lot, the golden rule is:

● clothes worn next to your skin should be washed after each wear.

It goes without saying that underwear should be changed regularly.

Regular hygiene checklist

Do you:

Bath or shower regularly?

Use an anti-perspirant/deodorant?

Check your nails for cleanliness?

Cut/file them to keep neat and tidy?

Regularly wash your hair?

Trim beard/moustache or shave each day?

Clean your teeth regularly?

Wash your clothes regularly?

Things to do before you start work

Prepare a list of 'things to do' before day one. Use the example below as a guide:

Fig. 13. Checklist: preparing for work.

THINGS TO DO

Before day one

1 Do you know bus/train times, where to park car/cycle? ☐

2 Do you have enough change for parking meter, tea, snacks? ☐

3 What clothes are you going to wear? Are they clean? ☐

4 Are your shoes clean? ☐

5 Make a list of things to take with you, eg, lunch, cup. ☐

On day one

6 Check out your personal hygiene. ☐

7 Check out your appearance. ☐

SURVIVING DAY ONE

Welcome to the world of work. Day One has arrived.

We'll assume your trip to work was incident free—you've arrived on time and it's time to enter the office.

Meeting the other staff

You may work in an office where the only staff member is the person who interviewed you. On the other hand, you may be joining several other staff who have been with the company for varying lengths of service.

No matter how many people work with you, they may not all have time to talk to you on Day One, but don't take it personally. Remember you have been chosen for the job above others who

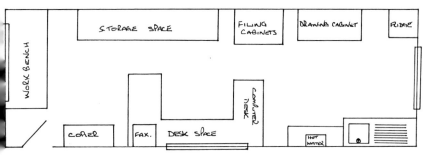

Fig. 14. Typical office arrangements in a small one person business.

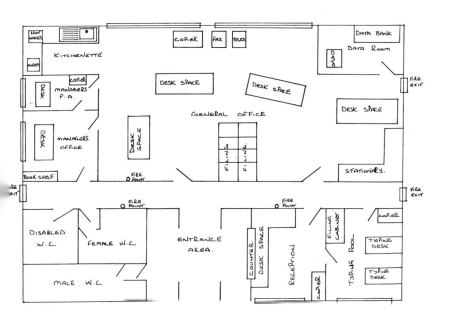

Fig. 15. Typical layout of a general office.

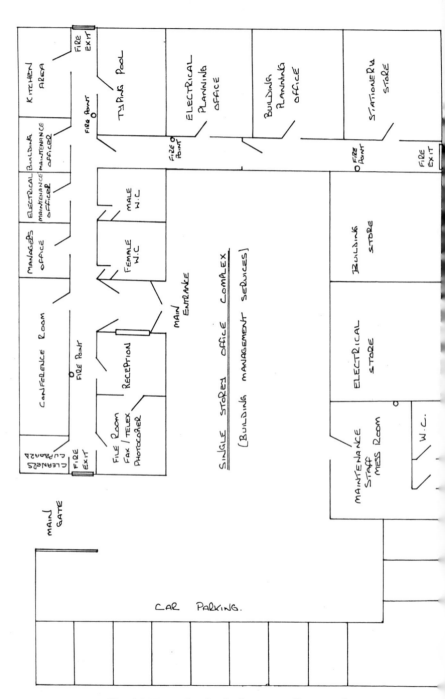

Fig. 16. Example of a single storey office complex.

applied for the same position. Even though you may not arrive to a grand reception committee, your presence is both welcome and needed. Most offices are very busy, especially on a Monday morning, so don't be put off if you are left to your own devices for a while.

Example
Imagine your first day at work—for the first hour your boss is answering the telephone, opening the mail and trying to deal with an irate customer who is making a complaint.

You sit quietly at your desk—you haven't a clue what you're supposed to do. Your options could include the following:

- do nothing, but throw dirty looks at your boss for not instructing you properly;

- have a go at using the typewriter;

- discreetly offer to make a drink and ask if there's anything you could do to help.

It is not unknown for inexperienced office workers to throw in a perfectly good job on the first day because they fail to understand the pressure other people are under. 'It was so boring, and he never gave me anything to do all day,' is a complaint which is unjustified. Can you imagine why an employer would go through the hassle of advertising, interviewing and employing new staff if they weren't needed?

Take your time
Don't try to become 'one of the lads' straight away. First impressions do not always give a true impression—your first week will be a time for you and the other staff to check each other out and, hopefully, develop a good working relationship. Therefore, don't be too pushy or too sure of yourself. Your manner could irritate and cause friction.

Example
Michael has always had a bit of a problem with other people. He can't understand why they get so annoyed with him.

While working with the four other staff, Claire, the receptionist, drops some sheets of paper she has just photocopied. Bending down to pick them up, she began to bristle with anger. It wasn't the fact she'd dropped the paper—it was the sound of Michael sniggering behind her that really wound her up.

Throughout the day, Michael's sniggering could be heard each time someone made a mistake. By the end of the day all three staff walked out the door without acknowledging Michael, who was quite upset by their attitude to him.

'If he sniggers at me again,' complained Claire to a colleague as she walked out of the door, 'I swear I'll ring his neck.'

When Michael arrived home he felt that he had done everything to make himself at home. 'I did everything I could to help people,' he moaned to his mother. 'But they're all so ungrateful—never even said good night to me!'

Just a simple habit Michael had carried with him from childhood, had isolated him from the workforce on his very first day. If you feel the other staff don't particularly like you, it may be something as simple as sniggering at the wrong time!

Be guided by other staff

Although you should use your initiative, you should also allow yourself to be guided by other staff who have more experience than you. You don't want to be known as a 'know-it-all' after your first week. Some people have a habit of trying too hard, which tends to be more annoying than helpful.

Ask where you should sit. Don't assume the empty chair by the computer is for you. It's owner may not appreciate you keeping his/her chair warm while they are out of the office.

Example
People are particularly possessive about their chair, their desk, their typewriter. If your brother sister or best friend went into your bedroom while you were away and borrowed your favourite shoes, bringing them back damaged, you would probably feel angry, even if you didn't show it.

Sitting down in a chair which has been used by the same person for several years is a similar invasion of their space. You may think it's only a chair, but to its 'owner', it's their property and their space.

Note the "pecking order"

There is alway an order of seniority, even if it is unofficial. You, as the latest recruit, will be at the bottom of the line to begin with. Whether you rise to the next rung is up to you. It may take you a couple of years (especially as staff now tend to stick to one employer as finding other employment is difficult) and you will have to prove yourself by your own efforts at work. You won't get promotion if you don't deserve it.

Example
On returning to work after several years, Rose, 36, soon settles into the routine. The two younger women—Emma, 19, and Imogen, 20—have been with the company since joining as YT trainees, but as they are younger than Rose, she assumes she is senior to them.

'Make us a cup of tea, Emma,' she asks towards the end of week one.

'Make it yourself,' retorts Emma. 'I've got to do this bank reconciliation by lunch time.'

The two have taken a dislike to each other, mainly because Rose assumed her place in the pecking order was higher because of her age. Emma is unused to being given the order to make tea as the staff all make their own when they feel like it.

Watch and observe
You learn a lot from observing others, by listening to them answering the telephone or dealing with customers. However, try not to copy bad practices. This book is designed to help you become good at your job and therefore, you need to be selective as to which skills you imitate and which you avoid like the plague.

Example
If you notice one of your colleagues regularly making telephone calls home to his new wife, would you assume it's OK to make personal calls whenever you feel like it? If another colleagues regularly cuts up unwanted letters and documents to use as note pads, would you copy this practice?

Make notes for future reference
Write down anything you think is important, or what you think you may forget, for example:

- 'I always take my coffee black with two sugars.'

- 'The stationery supplier calls on Thursdays—can you make sure you have a list of anything you need so that I can check it on Wednesday afternoon.'

- 'Mrs Tapp is one of our best customers. If she visits the office, make sure you contact me right away.'

Ask questions when appropriate

You should know where the fire exit and assembly point is in case of fire. If it is not clearly marked, ask. Be responsible for your own health and safety at work.

When you start working, if there is anything you don't understand, ask. Don't bravely plod on if you are typing a letter and can't understand your boss's writing, or file a document in the miscellaneous file because you can't figure out which one it really belongs in.

If you have used a photocopier before and have said so, don't keep it to yourself if you don't understand how to use the model your new employer has.

Don't make a nuisance of yourself

Don't become obsessional about Health and Safety and quote the regulations to your new employer. He will be well aware of them himself.

Read through work and mark all the words you cannot read and ask your boss for help *at one session* . . . don't go back each time you find a query, because on the tenth occasion you disrupt him, he might get more than a little annoyed.

Example

'I notice there's a frayed carpet in the stock room. According to Health and Safety Regulations, that's dangerous and could cause an accident. Something should urgently be done about it.'

The fact that the stock room is only a cupboard and the carpet was an off-cut stuck to the bottom, probably means no-one walks into the cupboard anyway. They are highly unlikely to trip over the frayed edge. Being aware of health and safety is important. Being a pain by forcing your views on other staff when you're being unrealistic isn't.

You're learning all the time

By the end of Day One you should have learned quite a lot, but you may not realise it. You probably know how to use a variety of equipment in the office and where the pens and stationery are kept. You should know the approved way to answer the telephone by listening to other staff and may know how to set out letters in line with company specifications.

Be positive

Go home and relax! You have made it through your first day. Be positive about what you have learned and look forward to tomorrow. Avoid moaning to your mum and dad or friends about the things you didn't like:

'They made me answer the 'phone—I hate answering the 'phone.'

Be positive about the things you have learned and the tasks you did well:

'I had to type out an invoice, and worked out the VAT myself. When my boss checked it, all the calculations were right!'

SMALL BUSINESSES—IT'S JUST YOU AND THE PHONE

If you work for a small company, you may be the only other office worker apart from your boss. She/he has employed you because they are confident you can do the job and you will probably work very closely with them.

In small businesses, it is not unusual for the boss to be the salesman/accountant/labourer as well. She/he will often have to leave you in charge of the office to see customers and other visitors. So what happens if on Day One he is called out and leaves you on your own?

The first thing to do is remember not to panic. Small companies rely on the boss to generate more business, entertain customers, check work out on site, as well as work in the office. You are not being put upon if you are left alone. It is unfortunate if it happens on Day One, but it's not the end of the world.

Prepare before starting work

If you know the boss is going out, ask him what he wants you to do while he's away. He'll probably say, 'Just answer the phone and take messages. I'll call them back—and you could do a bit of cleaning up. Just make yourself at home.'

You will probably wonder how on earth you can clean up a bit if you don't know where anything goes. However, if you are going to be the only staff member apart from the boss, it is likely you will eventually do almost everything regarding administration, so why not start on Day One by finding out for yourself?

You could suggest you sort out the files, 'so I know where things go.' Or you could ask if there is anything urgent which needs typing. While there is no-one around, it's an excellent time to get to know your typewriter/word processor . . . time when no-one's there to see you make the inevitable errors!

Make notes

Make a note of anything your boss tells you. For instance: 'By the way, I'm expecting a call from National Timbers. Can you make a note of the prices they're quoting?' Don't try to remember messages —write them down.

Questions you need answers to before the boss disappears

People store things in the most peculiar places. To save you time hunting for something which may be right beneath your nose, there are several things you need to know before your boss disappears.

Understanding the filing system

In what order are documents stored? Would the boss mind if you checked out the filing cabinet and organised it if necessary?

Ask where the user manuals are kept

If you are alone with an unfamiliar typewriter it is handy to have a user manual to guide you. If you are using a word processor, a user manual is essential, unless you have used that particular programme/ computer before.

If the boss has time, ask her/him to run through the booting-up (starting the computer) procedures, and show you which disks you can use to practise on. If she/he hasn't got the time, it's down to you.

Most word processors carry out the same functions: creating, editing, saving and printing documents. Leave emboldening, centring and underlining until you have more time to practise.

If you are having problems on any of the functions, find something else to do and leave it until the boss returns. You don't want to damage the computer, or wipe disks containing work documents.

If you have never used a computer before, it would be best if you wait until your boss is in the office before you 'play'. She/he will probably have discussed this with you at your interview, and you would be wise to wait for some expert instruction. Some employers send their staff for training or get an expert to give tuition.

What if there are no manuals?

Just hope that the boss or another member of staff knows how to use the computer, and your predecessor didn't take the knowledge with her. If there is no chance of finding the lost manual, contact a computer specialist and ask if they could locate a copy.

Who opens the mail?

You will have to know whether the boss prefers to open the mail himself. Some employers do this themselves through necessity, but there is no reason why you can't volunteer, If, however, the boss prefers to do it himself, don't push it. Once he gets to know you and can see how efficient you are, he may hand over the task to you at a later date.

If you do open the mail, make sure you deal with it correctly. There is additional information on the correct way to handle mail in the next chapter.

Do you take messages or ask the caller to ring back?

Some bosses prefer to get callers to ring them back at a time when they are certain to be in the office. This will save money on the telephone bill, but it may deter a prospective customer from calling back again. Others prefer to get the caller to leave a message and 'phone number so they can be contacted on the boss's return. It may be more expensive, telephone-wise, but new business could be gained by the return call.

Where can the boss be reached in an emergency?

There are times when the boss needs to be contacted about an urgent matter you simply cannot handle on your first day.

Example
It is extremely bad luck if the Health and Safety Inspector decides to spot-check the premises on Day One, or the security alarm is accidentally activated and you don't know the number to turn it off.

Only contact the boss if you see no other way out of a situation. Don't 'phone her/him up because you've run out of tea and want permission to use some petty cash money. The boss will not be amused.

Ask where resources are kept and where to purchase new ones

Resources can be anything from A4 paper, envelopes to new ribbons for your typewriter. You need to know what stock is available, and, if you are short of items, where to purchase them from. However, don't put in an order for £50 of stationery without first checking with the boss. You could, however, make note of what you have, what you need and new items you think should be added to your stock list.

Where's the kettle?

Hopefully, there will be a kettle and facilities for making tea or coffee. Ask if it will be OK to make yourself a drink. The boss probably won't mind. After all, by mid morning, with all the cleaning, answering the telephone and typing, you'll need a break!

YOU'RE ON YOUR OWN

Take a breather and have a cup of tea

Once the boss has left the office, it is really up to you to get yourself organised. If you are going to work on your own, you must organise yourself and the office from Day One. Organising the boss is another area, which will take time and patience, and a great deal of tact! But one step at a time.

Make a cup of tea, sit down, and plan your day.

Planning your day

You have to decide what you are going to do first, or you will find yourself doing a bit of this, a bit of that, and not really getting very far. However, don't tie yourself down to strict time constraints, or you'll give yourself a headache! And remember the length of your list will depend on the size of the company. It could be two items long, or cover a sheet of A4 paper.

Example objectives list

1 Check filing cabinet and tidy files—make note of how work was previously typed.
2 Check equipment to see if in good working order.
3 Use the typewriter/computer and type up notes.
4 Check stock and make list of items to order.
5 Type up list of queries.
6 Vacuum floor and polish desks.
7 10.00 and 2.30 Tea breaks.
8 12.00–1.00 Lunch.

Work out priorities

Only by checking will you be able to work out what your priorities will be in the office. If your first reaction when you walk in is to note how clean and tidy the office is, then vacuuming will be low on your priorities list. If the filing tray is brimming full of documents which have been dealt with, then filing will probably be pretty high.

Check out the filing system

If you have decided filing is your first priority and the boss has no objections to you reorganising, the easiest way to start is to clear your desk. Remove everything, so you have a clear surface to work on.

Look at the file tabs to see how the filing cabinet is classified:

- Is it alphabetical under customer names?

- Is it numercial under reference numbers?

- Is it in chronological order under dates?

- If the cabinet has no logical sequence, it may be that your boss knows where she/he can put her/his hands on the files, but doesn't know how to classify them. If you plan to reorganise the cabinet, make sure you write a note or memo to explain things to her/him.

Take out one file at a time from the front of the cabinet and check the file tab. Lay the contents on your desk and see if contents relate to the title. Other things to check are:

1 Are all the documents from the same company?

2 Are all the documents about the same subject, ie invoices, credit notes, contracts, quotations?

3 Is there nothing which ties them together at all?

If the contents tie in with the label, you are half way there. Now deal with the contents as follows:

1 If the documents are from the same company, file them in date order, most recent on the top.

2 If the documents are about the same subject, file them in date or numerical order if you think it appropriate, alphabetical if not.

3 If the documents are in no particular order, this may be the miscellaneous/other/sundry file—in other words, the file which is used for documents which have no file of their own. You may be able to file them in a logical sequence—see Chapter 5 on filing.

When you are happy with the filing system you can close the drawer and get on with the rest of your day—if there is anything left of it!

Familiarise yourself with equipment

Equipment can cover anything from a stapler or paper shredder to photocopier or computer. Check to see all equipment works, and make note of anything you don't know how to use, or suspect is broken/in need of repair.

Example

Shaun was trying to use the hole punch. No matter how he tried, he couldn't get the thing to work. Eventually, after half an hour, he asked someone—and they showed him how to release the safety catch!

Some simple equipment appears to be broken when there is a reason why it won't work. Even if you have used similar equipment at college, school or a previous job, there may be a simple reason why you can't get it to work for you.

Look at previous typed work for preferred layout and style

If you have passed a typing examination, you may or may not be impressed by your predecessor's layout of work. If you are a qualified typist and feel your style is better and layout neater, mention this tactfully to the boss and ask if he/she would mind the change. Some companies still use the indented method (see Chapter 5—section on typing styles) and may not want to change. If so, you will have to keep in line with the company preference.

Do a stock take of resources

Make note of everything in the office you will use and need to replace on a fairly regular basis. The list could look similar to the one in fig. 17 but may have more or less items.

Once your list is complete, you will see exactly what you have available and what you need to re-order. Prepare a list for your employer and discuss it with him at an appropriate time, ie when he's had time to sort out more important matters, such as returning telephone calls and checking the mail.

Make a note of other queries needing answers

Your list of queries at the end of the day will probably be growing by the minute. Therefore, make sure it is clear and to the point. Don't

OFFICE SUPPLIES LIST	Date:	
ITEM	NUMBER IN STOCK	NUMBER TO ORDER
Pens		
Pencils		
Ruler		
Tippex and thinner		
Eraser		
Typewriter ribbons		
Typewriter lift-off tapes		
Stapler/staples		
Paper clips		
Rubber bands		
Labels		
Envelopes		
A4 plain paper		
Compliment slips		
Headed notepaper		
Carbon paper		
Notepads		
Telephone message pads		
Petty cash vouchers		
Order forms		
Invoices		
Credit Notes		
Statements		
Toner for photocopier/printer		
Padded envelopes/Jiffy bags		
Parcel tape		
Glue/glue-sticks		

Fig. 17. An office supplies stock/order list.

throw all the questions at the boss as soon as she/he walks in. For more typing practice, type up the list neatly. And remember—even though it is only a list for yourself, you should take a pride in your work at all times. Your boss may want a copy . . . and you don't want him to see poorly prepared work!

Talk to the boss at the end of the day—admit mistakes!

The boss will probably ask how you have settled in. You can update him with your progress, go through your action lists and clear up any queries. You should also admit to any mistakes you have made.

'I'm afraid I've locked the filing cabinet and can't find the key.'

'I was cleaning up and dropped your cup. The handle broke off, I'm afraid.'

'A man called this morning. He said he'd ring back, and I forgot to get his name.'

No-one is perfect, and no-one expects you to get everything right the first time. Hopefully, you have made it on your own on Day One without any major disasters and you should congratulate yourself for coping so well. Think positively—and look forward to Day Two.

DAY TWO

More familiarisation with work

One Day Two you will have some idea of what to expect. But don't take it for granted that each day will be the same. Each day at work you will be learning new skills or improving the ones you already have and remember:

If a job's worth doing
it's worth doing well

END OF WEEK ONE

At the end of your first week, you will be well on your way to becoming part of the staff team, or your boss's right-hand person. However, if you feel as though you aren't fitting in, that going to work is a nightmare, try to work out why you feel that way.

List down all the things you like about the job and all the things you don't. Try to pin-point the problem and do something about it.

Examples
Problem solving list 1

Likes	Dislikes
Typing letters	Answering the phone
Making the tea	Talking to customers
Tea break	Lunch time
The boss	Using the computer
	Filing
	The woman from Accounts

Now analyse your dislikes and try to work out what it is about them that makes you feel bad.

Problem solving list 2

Dislike	Why
Answering phone	Nervous—don't like talking to people I don't know.
Talking to customers	Same reason as answering the phone.
Lunch time	Don't know what to do—spend hour walking round the shops.
Using the computer	Not sure how to work it properly. Rather use typewriter.
Filing	I have to do all the filing and it's boring.
Woman in Accounts	I know she doesn't like me, and I don't like her. She talks to me as though I were a kid.

When you know what it is you don't like, and why, then comes the hard part—working out what to do about the problem. You can talk to your boss about it, but first, why not try to work it out for yourself.

Problem solving list 3

Dislike	What can I do about it?
Answering the phone	I know I'm getting better on the phone. But I have to give myself more time to become confident.
Talking to customers	When I get to know them better, and have worked here longer, I will be able

	to answer their queries without becoming tongue-tied.
Lunch time	I'll ask the boss if I can sit in the office at lunch time and read or write a couple of letters to friends. Perhaps I'll ask the other girl in the office if she would like to come down the shops with me.
Using the computer	I need some practice. I wonder if the boss would let me use it at lunch time so I can get used to it?
Filing	I know it's my job, and I know it has to be done. Not much I can do about it.
The woman from Accounts	She's worked in the office for years, and has got two grandchildren my age. Maybe that's why she treats me like a kid. Perhaps if I didn't wind her up so much, and give her dirty looks all the time, she might be a bit nicer to me.

Some problems are out of your hands, and there is very little you can do about them, but always try to be positive about every situation. In a perfect world, talking about problems is the first step to solving them. Unfortunately, it isn't always that simple. If you know what the problem is, however, you are halfway there.

When do I get paid?

You may be paid at the end of your first week (wages) or monthly (salary). You may be paid in cash, by cheque or directly into the bank. There is nothing to beat the feeling of receiving your first week's wages and knowing you have worked to earn it.

If you are paid a week in hand, you may not receive your wages until the end of Week Two. But don't worry—the company do not keep your money, they simply hold it (in hand) until such time as you leave, are made redundant or laid off, and at that time, you will receive your wages, plus your first week's pay as well.

END OF MONTH ONE

By the end of the first month you should have settled in, ironed out initial problems with others, and know how to do your job reasonably, if not perfectly, well. Now is the time to look forward, and become an expert.

Some companies take on their employees for a month's or three months' trial. If you are in that position, remember you are still on probation and you must work to win a permanent place on the staff.

Remember who's boss

No matter how much you learn at work, the most important thing to remember is:

the boss is the boss.

If your employer wants to take a two-hour business lunch, spend the afternoon on the golf course with a business associate, it really is up to him. He is the boss because he has worked hard to get there. Don't tittle-tattle and moan because he arrives later in the office than you, or because one of the firm's suppliers gives him a free bottle of whiskey for Christmas. As they say, it's the perks of the job . . . and he is the boss.

CASE STUDIES

Lee

Lee has only just arrived on Day One. Because his father works for the company, he wants to appear confident and is already talking to the boss as though he were an old friend.

'Hello, Mr Davenport,' Lee says, with a little too much familiarity. 'Better make a cup of tea before we start.'

'I'd rather you wait for a cup of tea until the mail has been opened and we've done a bit of work.' Mr Davenport isn't too happy. He usually has a cup of tea around 10 o'clock, getting in a good hours work beforehand.

'That won't take me five mintes,' Lee enthusiastically picks up the mail and rips it open without much thought to the contents.

'Leave it!' says Mr Davenport abruptly, glaring at Lee. 'Just leave the mail where it is. Just sit over there,' he says, pointing to a chair by the desk set aside for Lee. 'Just sit there, and wait until I give you some work.'

'Sorry, I was only trying to help.' Lee can't understand why Mr Davenport is so moody.

Chriss

Chriss walks into the office on Day One. Her new boss, Mr Roberts, is waiting for her. 'Look, I'm sorry about this, but I've got to visit a client, and will be gone most of the day. I'm sorry to leave you in the lurch. Have a good look round and I'll see you about three this afternoon.'

Chriss is very nervous, but doesn't let it show. 'That's OK. I'm sure I can cope. Can I just ask you a few things before you disappear?' she asks, as Mr Roberts pushes papers frantically into his briefcase.

Chris asks several practical questions:

- Is there a telephone number where Mr Roberts can be contacted in an emergency?

- Where are the user manuals for the computer?

- Is there anything urgent which needs to be dealt with today?

Mr Roberts quickly answers her questions, and rushes out the door.

Chriss takes a deep breath, and begins to familiarise herself with her new environment. By the time Mr Roberts returns, the office is clean and tidy . . . and Chriss has sorted the files!

Jackie

Jackie has started work and is very unsure of herself. She has been asked to photocopy some brochures and type a letter.

She manages the photocopying, but has problems with the letter. Each time she comes across a word she is unsure of, she asks her boss. After the seventh interruption, Mr Eliot's temper is getting a little frayed.

'For God's sake, Jackie! Can't you read the letter through and circle all the words you can't read? Then I can tell you them all at once and get on with this damn report.'

Jackie apologises, near to tears.

'It's your first day,' Mr Eliot says kindly, realising he may have been too abrupt. 'But I'm really busy. You've got to start thinking for yourself—you're not at school now.'

Jackie reads through the rest of the letter, managing to sort most of it out herself. She only checks once more with Mr Eliot before finishing the letter. She feels really pleased with herself when he signs the letter and praises her for her perfect typing.

SUMMARY

Prepare yourself for work before Day One
- travel
- money
- clothes
- what to take
- personal hygiene

Working for a company with more than one staff
- be guided by other staff
- watch and observe
- make notes for future reference
- ask questions when appropriate
- don't make a nuisance of yourself

Just you and the boss
- ask questions
- plan your day
- work out priorities
- familiarise yourself with equipment and files
- check out typing style
- stock take resources
- make list of queries
- talk to the boss and admit mistakes

POINTS FOR DISCUSSION

1   Can you think of two advantages of working for a small company, and two of working for a larger concern? Which would suit your personality more?

2   Do you understand the meaning of 'using your initiative'? Check it in the dictionary if you don't.
     Give two examples of how you have used your initiative over the past week. If you can't give examples, think of two ways in which you could use your initiative at home, eg washing up without being asked!

3   How would you react in Jackie's position? How do you react to constructive criticism—do you accept it without losing your temper, or do you storm off in a mood, looking like thunder?
     If you tend to be moody/lose your temper quickly, how does your reaction make you feel—better or worse?

5
Basic Office Duties

The following basic duties are not in any set order, but you may find yourself involved in any of them at the beginning of your employment. There are right and wrong ways to deal with all of them—these are one way, which you could use as your guide.

Summary of duties:

- answering the phone and greeting visitors

- photocopying

- mail-handling

- filing

- typing

- word processing

- data processing

- dealing with money

- banking

- business transactions

ANSWERING THE TELEPHONE AND GREETING VISITORS

First impressions should be the right impressions.

Quite often the receptionist or person answering the phone is the first line of contact for prospective customers. Therefore, first impressions should be the right impressions. It takes about four minutes for a customer to form an opinion of you, so always be polite, cheerful and helpful.

Telephone answering skills

When answering the telephone remember the following:

- Always have a pen and piece of paper or notepad/telephone mesage pad by the telephone. Answer quickly, before the fourth ring (the national standard).

- Speak clearly and with a smile. 'Good morning, Smith and Co. How can I help you?' spoken with a cheery voice will give the caller more confidence than a gruffly spoken 'Mornin', Smiths.'

- Always say 'Good morning' or 'Good afternoon' first. These two words give the caller a chance to tune into what you are saying. Follow this by your company name and perhaps 'Can I help you?', or 'How may I help you?'

- Listen to the caller and make note of their name—write it on your pad to help you remember. Ask for the spelling if you don't quite catch it.

- Try to be as helpful as you can, and don't leave the caller hanging on for long periods without coming back to them. If you have to look for someone, or something to answer a query, the waiting time for the caller will pass by slowly. If necessary, go back to the caller and apologise—and don't just say 'sorry to keep you waiting' and immediately put the 'phone down again. Listen to their response. If you don't give them the chance to reply, they will feel very frustrated and annoyed . . . and eventually, when you return to the 'phone, they may not be too happy!

- If you take a message, ensure you have all the details. You need the name of the caller, his/her telephone number and the message. Write down the time of the call, date and your signature:

  Time—so the person receiving the message will know what time of day the caller rang.

  Date—the receiver may not be in the office that day, and it must be clear when the message was received.

  Your signature—if the message is unclear, the receiver then knows who took it. They can check the details with you . . . and instruct you on how to take a message properly.

Telephone message pad are ideal—they give prompts on what to ask the caller. However, it doesn't always follow that you ask the right questions, even with a message pad at your side.

Example

The 'phone rings and you're alone. You know you should answer it before the fourth ring but you just can't get yourself to pick it up. Eventually the caller rings off. You know you have to answer it the next time, and hope the caller thinks he dialled the wrong number before.

Write down exactly what you should say on a piece of scrap paper and keep it by the 'phone. Say it to yourself several times—if there's noone in the office it won't matter if you talk to yourself.

When the 'phone rings again, take a deep breath and pick up the receiver. Read your message slowly. 'Good morning, Dice Services. Can I help you?' If you don't remember to smile as you speak the first time, it's OK. Just work on your technique each time you answer the following callers.

Listen to the caller carefully. Find out what they want and make notes to help you remember.

The next time you answer, it really will be a little easier.

Fig 18 is an example of a typical telephone message pad:

TELEPHONE MESSAGE PAD

To: . . . .   while you were out

M . . . .   Date: . . . .

Of . . . .   Time: . . . .

Tel No: . . . .   Initials: . . . .

Message: . . . .

. . . .

. . . .

. . . .

. . . .

Telephoned	Please ring	Called to see you
Will call again	Wants to see you	Urgent

Fig. 18. Example of a telephone message pad.

Summary

1 Be polite, cheerful and helpful.
2 Answer the telephone before fourth ring.
3 Have a pen and paper handy.
4 Smile when you speak.
5 Listen to caller.
6 Write clear, accurate messages.

PHOTOCOPYING

This may only seem like a minor task but it should be done with care. Paper for the photocopier should be stored in a flat, dry place, as creased or damp paper may jam the machine.

Poorly photocopied material gives a bad impression, especially if you are sending it out to customers. To ensure your copies are good, the following should be remembered:

- Always position your original copy carefully. A few millimetres out, and a black line will show up on the edge of the copy.

- Check the original is of a good, clear quality. If the copy is too light or dark, most copiers have the facility to adjust the tone. However, if your original copy is too poor, it will be difficult to improve on.

- Dark paper (dark red, blue or orange) makes poor copy. No matter how you adjust your copier, the copy will probably be dark grey or black in colour.

- If the original copy has been corrected with Tippex, make sure it is dry before placing the copy face down on the copier. Wet fluid leaves blotches on the glass which show as a grey mark on the copy. Always clean the copier when you have finished—your colleagues won't be happy if they too have grey marks on their copies.

- If your original is of good quality and your copy is still poor (even after adjustment), your toner (a black powder) may be running low. If you don't know how to refill the copier, get someone to show you. NOTE: The black toner powder is almost impossible to remove from clothing. Be very careful when handling it. If it does get on your clothes, brush it off lightly. If you rub at it, it will embed itself in the fabric and will be with your garment forever!

- If the copy hasn't improved, you may have to have your machine serviced. Most copiers are hired and the service is part of a contract. If the photocopier is owned by your employer, a service may be expensive. Check to see if there is anyone in the company who knows how to clean the copier before doing anything else.

Copier not working?

Finally, if the copier won't work at all, check the following:

- Is it plugged in and switched on?

- Has the paper run out? Don't forget to fan the paper (separate the sheets) before putting more into the copier. More copiers jam because of sheets of paper sticking together than any other reason.

- Are all parts of the copier are closed? If the front panel is left partly open, or the paper tray isn't pushed in far enough, the copier won't operate.

- Has the toner run out? Usually a red or orange light will give an indication if this has happened.

Check with your copier manual if you cannot sort out a problem, or call your dealer.

One more important thing to remember about photocopying is the **copyright law**. This is designed to protect authors or anyone who has produced some original work, from having it copied by others without their permission. In other words, if material has the © sign, don't photocopy it unless you have permission from the author. The law applies to copying photographs, recording records (from the radio, record, CD or tape), as well as to books, information sheets, scripts, songs, and similar material. There is an example of the © copyright sign at the front of this book.

Example
Imagine you have just written a short story about your experiences on holiday. You let a friend have a copy as she is impressed with your writing skills.

Two months later, you see a story identical to yours. It's been published in *Just 17* and your friend has been acknowledged as the author.

What could you have done to stop this from happening?

Summary
1   Store paper carefully.
2   Position paper accurately and check original of good quality.
3   Remember the Copyright Law.
4   Avoid spilling toner on clothes.

HANDLING THE MAIL

One of the first tasks of the morning should be to open and distribute the incoming mail. Letters, invoices, orders, requests for quotes, remittances and brochures all call for some sort of action by the office worker.

Larger companies may have their own Post Room. Unless you work in that particular department you may not come into contact with the mail at all.

If you work for a small company, however, you may well be asked to open and sort the mail. Make this a priority task. If the mail arrives after you, don't leave it sitting on your desk until tea break—open it as soon as possible.

Opening and distributing incoming mail
If you are given the job of sorting the mail and someone has instructed you as to how this should be carried out, stick to the organisational policy. Make notes and refer to them during the first few days or until you are familiar with them.

If you work for a large company you may be given an organisation chart—this lists job titles and the names of people working in those departments. If a chart is not available, make one of your own. Find out who works for which department and what goes on there. If in doubt—ask questions.

Organisation charts
If you would like to make an organisation chart of your own, the example in fig. 19 will give you an idea of how to do it.

Before opening the mail
If there is no-one to instruct you, use the following information to help:

1   Some letters have to be signed for, ie, Registered or Recorded Delivery. Before signing, check the correspondence is actually addressed to your company.

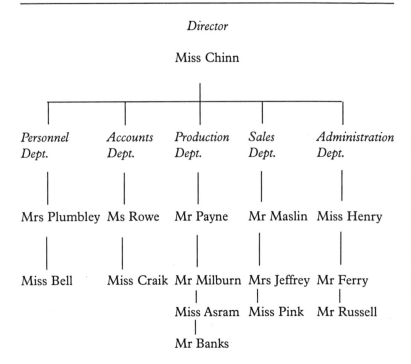

Fig. 19. An organisation chart, showing the functions of the business, and the staff responsible.

2   Check all envelopes before opening—the correspondence may have been delivered to the wrong address. Letters delivered to the wrong address should be re-posted.

3   Private, personal and confidential letters should be delivered *unopened* to the appropriate person.

4   If the letter is addressed to a particular person by name, again deliver this unopened.

Opening the mail

1. Taking care
On opening the mail make sure you don't damage the contents. Use a paper-knife or a letter opener if one is available. If not, you may have to improvise—but take care, remember Health and Safety at Work—you're unlikely to cut yourself if you use a pen but you may if you use a penknife.

2. Check for enclosures

After opening the mail, check the contents carefully to see whether anything is enclosed. Enclosures may be indicated on letters they accompany as follows:

- Enc or Encs typed/written at the bottom of letters.

- Three full stops typed in the margin next to the mention of an enclosure.

- Read through the correspondence and see whether an enclosure is mentioned.

The enclosures could be anything from cheques to invoices or brochures. If an enclosure isn't with the accompanying letter, make a note of this on the correspondence and tell your employer.

Staple or paper-clip enclosures to the accompanying correspondence.

3. Record the date

Date-stamp all mail or write the date on it. This will help for future reference, especially if there is no date on the correspondence.

4. Incoming Mail book

If you have an Incoming Mail book, record all correspondence for future reference (see fig. 20).

Example Your employer has just received a 'phone call from a supplier. The supplier has threatened to close your company's account because an invoice he sent two months ago has not been paid. You check your Incoming Mail book for the past two months. The invoice was never received—your employer can now request a copy and hopefully save the account.

5. Basic sorting

You can now initially sort the incoming mail into two sections:
    Correspondence with payments enclosed
    All other correspondence

6. The Remittances Book

A Remittances Book is used to record payments received, whether they are in the form of cheques, postal orders or cash. Check that the payments are correct and the totals as stated in the accompanying

Date 199..	Sender	Contents	Passed to
2 Dec	I. Bell Ltd	Invoice	G. Webb
2 Dec	Lambourne End Centre	Statement	G. Webb
2 Dec	Southbourne Suppliers	Cheque	G. Webb
2 Dec	Dallalmore + Co	Order + Cheque	G. Webb
3 Dec	S Bowers Ltd	Ins. policy	B Houghton
3 Dec	Carole Roberts	Cheque	G. Webb

Fig. 20. Example of a page from an Incoming Mail Book.

letters. An example of a partly-completed Remittance Book is shown in fig 21. To remit' just means to 'send in' or 'to send back'.

7. Paying in remittances
Once the cheques, cash and postal orders have been recorded they should be removed from their correspondence and banked. If you know where the bank paying-in book is fill in a slip with details of all remittances. If you are unsure how to do this, see the section on Banking (page 112). Put the paying-in book and remittances safely away until you or someone else can get to the bank.

8. Coping on your own
If you are in the office on your own you may not be able to deal with any of the correspondence yourself, especially if you have only just started to work for the company. In this case it is best to place all mail on your boss's desk. He will deal with it when he comes in and tell you what to do.

9. Letters addressed to invidivuals
If some letters are addressed to a specific person in the company you can pass the correspondence on to them. If you are unsure who the mail is for, **check with someone** before leaving it on the wrong persons desk. Only experience will enable you to complete this task quickly and efficiently.

Date 199-	Remitter's Name	Method of Payment	Account No	Amount £	Balance £	Sig
2 Dec	Southbourne Suppliers	Cheque	07632	93.40	93.40	SP
2 Dec	Dallamore + co	Cheque	05873	36.50	129.90	SP
3 Dec	Carole Roberts	Cheque	06329	54.20	184.10	SP

Fig. 21. Extract from a typical Remittances Book.

10. Envelopes, stamps and clearing up
Before throwing envelopes away double-check you have left nothing in them. If possible, rip open the empty envelopes in case anything is stuck inside.

If someone in the company saves postage stamps for charity also remove these—you could always use one of the discarded envelopes to store them in.

Until you become more confident, your dealing with incoming mail may finish here. There is only one thing left to do now—clear up any mess you may have made.

Summary
For a summary of mail handling, see the flow chart of opening and distributing incoming mail (fig. 22).

Now try out the following incoming mail questionnaire—the answers can be found on page 170.

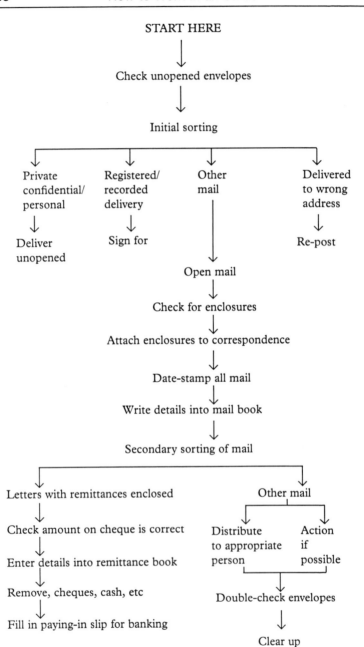

Fig. 22. A flow chart showing the steps to be taken for opening and distributing incoming mail.

Incoming mail handling: check your knowledge

1 What is a remittance?

. . . .

2 How would you deal with Private and Confidential mail?

. . . .

. . . .

3 Why should you date-stamp all mail?

. . . .

. . . .

4 If a letter is delivered to you but is addressed to another company, what would you do with it?

. . . .

. . . .

5 Can you name two things which show that something has been enclosed with a letter?

. . . .

. . . .

6 What do you write in a Remittances Book?

. . . .

. . . .

7 What details appear on an organisation chart?

. . . .

. . . .

8 What do the initials HASAW stand for?

. . . .

. . . .

9 What is a paying-in slip used for?

. . . .

. . . .

10   What should you do before throwing envelopes away?

. . . .

. . . .

Answers to incoming mail questionnaire are at the back of the book.

Preparing and despatching outgoing mail

Price lists of current postal rates are available from the Post Office. These give details of not only first and second class mail, but Registered and Recorded Delivery, parcel rates, international rates, etc.

Some companies have their own postage, or outgoing mail book where they keep a check on all outgoing mail. Similar to the incoming mail book (see fig. 23), it enables office staff to check when letters or parcels were sent if there is a query.

Mail room equipment

If the company sends out a lot of mail it may have a **franking machine**. Letters or labels are passed through the machine, which prints the cost of the postage and, sometimes the company's logo. The Post Office holds a key, which opens the machine. To fill up the franking machine it has to be taken to the Post Office, which enters

Date 199..	Sent to	Postage	Comments	Sig
14 Dec	M. Smith	·33		mc
14 Dec	Peach House	·64	Recorded Delivery	MC
14 Dec	Shelliff motors	·24		mc

Fig. 23. Extract from an Outgoing Mail Book.

new units on payment of money. The sum depends on how many units (usually 1p units) the company needs.

Other equipment could include:

- scales for weighing letters and parcels

- addressing machines for addressing envelopes

- collating machines for sorting and placing in order, sheets of photocopying to be sent out

- folding machines for the automatic folding of documents

- inserting and mailing machine which automatically opens the envelope, inserts the paperwork, seals the envelope and franks it with correct postage

- package tying machine for the automatic wrapping of parcels

- letter opening machine which cuts a sliver off the top of the envelope for easy opening.

Health and safety at work

In these days of terrorists and violence, you should know what to do if you have a suspicious parcel. It is highly unlikely this will ever happen, but *if* you genuinely are concerned about a packet, you should leave it where it is, evacuate the office and call the police by dialling 999. They will arrange for its removal and destruction, if necessary. However, they will not be impressed if you call them out on a false alarm for no very good reason.

Take care with sharp instruments such as scissors or knives when opening envelopes or parcels. Use staplers sensibly—don't play with them unless you want to staple your finger.

Avoid removing staples with your fingernails. Specially designed staple removers can be purchased quite cheaply and do the job quickly and efficiently. Avoid the sharp edge of paper. Licking envelopes may not appear to be a hazard, but you can cut your tongue on the paper's edge or, just as painfully, your finger. Paper cuts usually sting and can be fairly deep.

Example

Darren has opened the mail, separated the cheques from the rest of the letters, and written them into the remittance book. He has filled in a paying-in slip and is waiting for his boss, Mark, to collect them and take them to the bank.

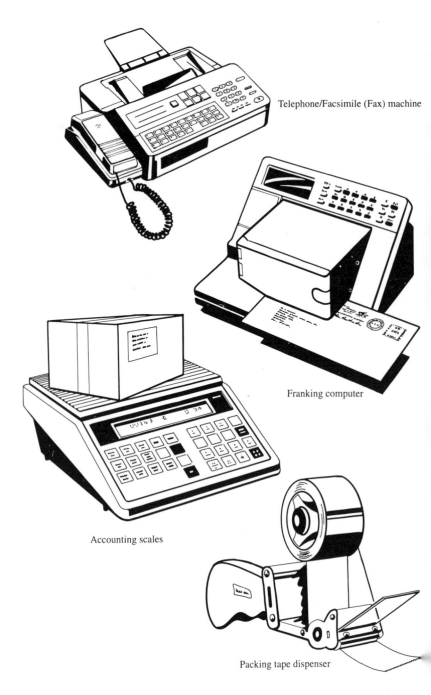

Telephone/Facsimile (Fax) machine

Franking computer

Accounting scales

Packing tape dispenser

Fig.24. Examples of mail room equipment.

Picking up the stapler, he starts to fire staples at the bin, trying to get four perfect shots in five seconds. 'Damn,' he mutters, as the stapler jams, unable to keep up with his firing speed. After unjamming the machine, he holds it in his hand, placing his index finger between the top at bottom, squeezing the stapler at the same time.

'Ouch.' Looking at his finger, a staple has firmly embedded itself in his finger. He removes it and blood gushes from the two pin-prick holes. It's only a small wound, but two days later he has to visit the doctor—his finger has turned septic.

FILING

Accurate filing is essential in an office and reference was briefly made to this in Chapter 4 and again in the mail handling section.

Filing should be done daily and with accuracy. Many documents are lost and time wasted through inefficient filing. Getting to grips with your filing system should, therefore, be a priority.

Types of filing

Type	Example
Alphabetical	Aldridge
	Brown
	Chinn
	Cutherbert
Numerical	05967
	06673
	08465
	09543
Chronological	1 May
	16 May
	23 May
	24 May
Geographical	Glamorgan, Pontypridd
	Glamorgan, Swansea
	Hampshire, Portsmouth
	Hampshire, Southampton
Subject	Brochures
	Equipment Manuals
	Furniture Price Lists
	Specifications

When you start work ask colleagues to go through the filing system with you or, if you are in the office on your own, go through the files yourself.

If you are starting a job as filing clerk in a small company and the files have been neglected, you may need to reorganise them (see Chapter Four on filing). Ask your employer and other staff if they have any objections; explain the system you would like to use.

Keep the system simple—you are not at work 24–hours a day and other staff may have to search the files for documents.

Regardless of the filing method used, the system is only as good as the person using it. The most frequently used files should be in the most easily accessible drawer; if you have to bend down to the lowest file many times during the day, you'll probably end up with back ache.

If you can't remember if N comes before M, simply write out your alphabet to use as a reference. Don't be embarrassed—it is better to get it right than to guess at it.

Never throw away documents if the files become full. Weed out documents over a year old and place them in a 'dead file'—an old A4 envelope can be used for this, but make sure you label it clearly with a thick marker pen, giving the year and contents.

The dead file should be kept for at least 5 years and can be stored in a cupboard or loft, where access is available should the papers be required for yearly audits or other investigations.

There are many text books which can help you learn about the different methods of filing and equipment used if you need further information—several are listed at the back of this book.

Types of filing equipment

Vertical filing is still one of the most commonly used, although computerised databases are now becoming a popular competitor. The list below covers some of the filing equipment available.

Vertical filing

Files are arranged upright and papers can be put in or taken out without removing the file from the cabinet. Plastic tabs are fitted to the top of the files making recognition of contents easy.

Electronic filing

A database can be set up to store vast amounts of information. Staff access the machine's memory and can produce a print-out of files on request. Quick and efficient, but requires some computer training. Data (information) is stored on disks or in the computer's memory.

Card index filing
A card index consists of a tray or box containing small cards. Information is typed or written on the cards. Often used for names, addresses and telephone numbers of clients. Guide cards separate the different sections.

Lateral filing
Files are arranged sidebyside and have to be removed to file documents. Titles are written vertically along the front of the files.

Plan filing
Large flat or vertical drawers are used to file plans and drawings. Files are divided into compartments and labelled with index strips for identification.

Microfilms
Used to store large amounts of information in a small space. Documents are filmed and stored on microfiche, cassettes or cartridges. A Micro Reading machine is necessary to view documents.

Fig. 25 is a flow chart showing filing procedures.

Health and safety at work
Even filing can be hazardous—most cabinets are made of metal and sharp edges can cut . . . especially if drawers are left open when not in use. Try to remember the following to cut down the chances of an accident:

- Don't leave drawers open, especially the lower ones—if the drawer is not above waist height, it may not be immediately noticeable—not until someone walks into it and bangs their shin.

- If the drawers are part-empty, try to spread the files inside so the weight is distributed throughout the drawer.

- If possible, put more weight in the lower files—if the cabinet is top-heavy, it may tip over when opened.

- Only open one drawer at a time to avoid the cabinet tipping forward (although some cabinets are designed to prevent you opening more).

Summary
1   Check filing system.
2   Sort and reorganise if necessary.

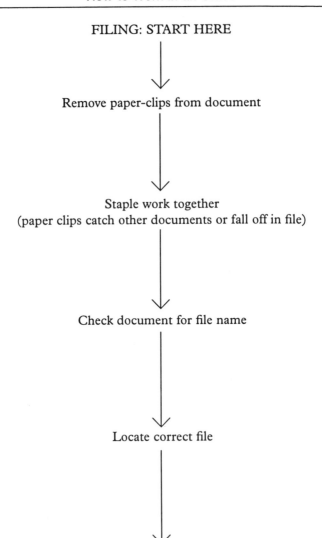

Fig. 25. A flowchart showing filing step-by-step.

3   Keep system simple.
4   File daily.
5   Write out alphabet if necessary.
6   Weed out old files and place in dead file.
7   Keep old files for five years.
8   Remember health and safety at work.

TYPING

If you have already gained a qualification in typing, you will know how to lay out most documents to an acceptable standard. You should also know how to correct them without leaving a hole in the document or smudgy finger-prints.

There are many different typewriters, and most good office equipment stores can give you a full list of what is available. As most companies already have a typewriter we won't list the different types here.

Proof reading

Some office juniors believe it is their employer's job to read through their work, mark errors and return the document for correction. They are wrong. Most employers don't have the time or the patience to do this, and a good typist reads through work, locates and corrects errors.

Always read through your work before removing it from the typewriter—it is far easier to locate the error and correct it if it is still in the machine. Proofread it again once the document has been removed.

The way to do this is to place the original document next to the typed copy. Run your fingers over both copies at the same time, checking each word carefully. Missing words, or incorrect information can be located; with practice the task can be done fairly quickly.

Use a dictionary to check any words you suspect to be incorrect. If you misspell the same word over and over again, type it on a card or piece of paper and place it inside your dictionary.

In fig. 26 a list of abbreviations and their meaning has been given. The list includes some of the most misspelled words in the office. With practice, your spelling can and will improve.

Example
Jo's boss has grown tired of pointing out her typing errors. His firm is expanding and his time is valuable. He lectures Jo on the necessity

SHARPEN UP YOUR OFFICE SKILLS!

Three great paperbacks to help you in your work

HOW TO MASTER BUSINESS ENGLISH
Michael Bennie

Are you communicating effectively? Do your business documents achieve the results you want? Or are they too often ignored or misunderstood? Good communication is the key to success in any business. Whether you are trying to sell a product, answer a query or complaint, or persuade colleagues, the way you express yourself is often as important as what you say. With lots of examples, checklists and questionnaires to help you, this book will speed you on your way. 'An excellent book – not in the least dull ... Altogether most useful for anyone seeking to improve their communication skills.' *IPS Journal.*

£7.99, 208pp illus. 0 7463 0582 6.

HOW TO WRITE A REPORT
John Bowden

Contents: Preparation and planning. Collecting and handling information. Writing the report: principles and techniques. Improving your thinking. Improving presentation. Achieving a good writing style. Making effective use of English. How to choose and use illustrations. Choosing paper, covers and binding. Appendices (examples, techniques, checklists), glossary, index. 'Most of us have a need to write a report of some kind at various times, and this book has real value ... Thoroughly commendable.' *IPS Journal.*

£7.99, 160pp illus. 1 85703 035 4.

HOW TO KEEP BUSINESS ACCOUNTS
Peter Taylor

A new revised edition of an easy-to-understand handbook for all business owners and managers. 'A clear step-by-step guide to accounting procedures.' *Mind Your Own Business.* 'Progresses through the steps to be taken to maintain an effective double entry book-keeping system with the minimum of bother.' *The Accounting Technician.* 'Compulsory reading.' *Manager, National Westminster Bank (Midlands).*

£8.99, 176pp illus. 1 85703 111 3. 3rd edition.

Please add postage & packing (UK £1.00 per copy. Europe £2.00 per copy. World £3.00 per copy airmail).
How To Books Ltd, Plymbridge House, Estover Road, Plymouth PL6 7PZ, United Kingdom. Tel: (0752) 695745. Fax: (0752) 695699. Telex: 45635.

accom	accommodation	hrs	hours
a/c(s)	account(s)	immed	immediately
ack	acknowledge	incon	inconvenient/ence
advert(s)	advertisement(s)	info	information
agt	agreement	inv.	invoice
altho'	although	Ltd	Limited (company)
appt(s)	appointment(s)	mfr(s)	manufacturer(s)
approx	approximate/ly	misc	miscellaneous
asap	as soon as possible	mm	millimetres
bel	believe	necy	necessary
b/f	brought forward	n.d	no date/not dated
bus	business	opp(s)	opportunity/ies
c	copy (or 'circa'—approx)	org	organisation
cc	copies	OTE	on-target earnings
c/f	carried forward	Paye	Pay as You Earn
cat(s)	catalogue(s)	PLC	public limited company
CEO	Chief Executive Officer	pl.	please
cm(s)	centimetre(s)	p/t	part time
co(s)	company/ies	poss	possible
cttee(s)	committee(s)	p.p.	per pro ('on behalf of')
comm	commission	re	as to, concerning
cr.	credit	rec(s)	receipt(s)
def	definite/ly	rec(d)	receive(d)
dept	department	ref(s)	reference(s)
dr.	debit	refd	referred
E.&O.E.	errors and omissions excepted	rep	representative
enc.	enclosed, enclosure	resp	responsible
ETA	exercise	sec(s)	secretary/ies
ex	executive	sep	separate
exec	expense(s)	s/h	shorthand
exp(s)	experience	sig(s)	signature(s)
exp	estimated time of arrival	suff	sufficient
f.a.o.	for attention of	temp	temporary
f/t	full time	thro'	through
f.y.i	for your information	t/w	typewriter, typewriting
gntee(s)	guarantee(s)	w.p.m.	words per minute
gov(s)	governments	y/e	year ended
HASAW	Health & Safety at Work		

Fig. 26. Some common business abbreviations to know.

to find her own errors as he just doesn't have the time any more. She agrees to try harder, and satisfied his 'chat' has done the trick, he doesn't bother to read through her work any more.

Unfortunately, Jo soon slips back into her old ways. Within a week her boss has received two complaints from customers about invoices they have received. One was charged for goods they haven't had and the other was charged the incorrect price.

As Jo was on a three-month trial basis, at the end of her time he decides not to keep her on and readvertises the position.

Methods of correcting typed work

There are several methods of correcting, but do make sure corrected errors are not clearly visible.

Lift-off tape

A tape fitted behind the typing ribbon. Cloudy-white in colour, it is slightly sticky and lifts off the print from the page. It cannot be used with a fabric ribbon. The tapes are fairly expensive, and can be re-wound and used again. If you do rewind your tape, keep it tightly wound and away from the 'feet'.

Liquid correcting fluid

This comes in a variety of colours, to match the paper. If a typing error is made, it can be painted out with the fluid, which should be bone-dry before retyping. If drying time isn't sufficient, the liquid may mark the typewriter, and is difficult to remove.

Always replace the lid, as exposure to air can cause the liquid to dry up. If the correcting fluid thickens, thinners can be added to thin it down. If the inside of the bottle lid becomes clogged with hardened liquid, remove it with a small screwdriver or similar tool—but be careful—and watch your hands (HASAW).

Correcting paper

Small, thin sheets of paper—coated on one side with a film of correcting powder. If an error is made, place the sheet of correcting paper in front of the typing key/daisy wheel and retype correctly. The original error is then covered with the powder. Not a good, permanent method of correction, as powder tends to rub off if the document is used regularly.

Typing eraser

A pencil-shaped rubber, hardened with pumice (volcano dust). A typing eraser is harder than a pencil eraser, so care should be taken not to make a hole in the paper through over-exuberant rubbing. Care should also be taken that dust doesn't fall into the typewriter, especially if you are using an electronic machine.

Layout of documents

It is not possible to show you the layout of all documents, but there are general rules you should stick to:

- Left-hand margin   this should always be at least an inch wide, and can be wider. It needs to be at least an inch to allow punching holes for filing.

- Right-hand margin   same size or smaller than the left-hand margin, but at least ½" wide.

- One space after
comma	= ,
semi-colon	= ;
dash	= -

- Two spaces after
full stop	= .
colon	= :
question mark	= ?
exclamation mark	= !

- Brackets   (as shown here) are spaced as per the example in this sentence.

1"	= 1 inch)	
2'	= 2 feet)	correct spacing for measurements
1 in	= 1 inch)	
2 ft	= 2 feet)	

- Paragraphs   return twice between each paragraph

- Headings   return twice between main and sub-headings

The following two letters in figs. 27 and 28 can be used as a guide for correct layout. The first is in the **fully blocked** style. This style is generally used today, and is quicker than the second example, the **indented style**.

The fully blocked method is far quicker and has a more modern look to it. Stick to this style unless your employer prefers the other method.

Always take a copy of documents (carbon or photocopy) for the files unless your employer tells you otherwise.

Our Ref SEP/JTO

15 April 199–

Mr T Powell
Frith Lane
Wickham
FAREHAM
PO18 4QG

Dear Mr Powell

RE: ORDER FOR PORTABLE APPLIANCE TESTING

Thank you for your letter regarding portable appliance testing.

We will be happy to visit your workshops on 26 April to test six portable appliances. We will issue a computer print-out of the results on site, and issue a certificate for appliances which come up to the national standard shortly after.

Please do not hesitate to contact me again should you require further information.

Yours sincerely
DICE SERVICES

Mr G Green

Fig. 27.   Example of a letter set out in fully blocked style. It is only punctuated in the body of the letter, not in the address, date, or signature.

Our Ref   SEP/JTO

15 April, 199–

Mr. T. Powell,
Frith Lane,
Wickham,
FAREHAM,
PO18 4QG

Dear Mr. Powell,

<u>RE: ORDER FOR PORTABLE APPLIANCE TESTING</u>

      Thank you for your letter regarding portable appliance testing.

      We will be happy to visit your workshops on 26 April to test six portable appliances. We will issue a computer print-out of the results on site, and issue a certificate for appliances which come up to the national standard shortly after.

      Please do not hesitate to contact me again should you require further information.

      Yours sincerely,
      DICE SERVICES,

      Mr. G. Green.

Fig. 28.   Example of a letter in indented style. It is punctuated from start to finish.

Example

'What on earth possessed you to type the Minutes like this?' your new employer asks. 'Didn't you think to check in the files? You haven't included an action column on any of the pages!'

'But that's the style I was taught. The RSA prefer a standard layout. I do know what I'm talking about because I passed my RSA II with Distinction.'

'I couldn't care less if you did. I need these Minutes this afternoon, and I want them typed my way.'

There is no point in arguing with your employer about the layout of documents. Although you have to follow certain rules to pass an examination, remember you have to follow certain rules to please your employer as well . . . and he pays your wages.

Envelopes

Often, window envelopes are used today when sending letters, invoices and statements. The 'window' (a see-through panel) means, if folded properly, that the address on the document can be seen through the panel, making it unnecessary to type out an envelope. Labels are also used, as these are quicker to type; the line of labels is inserted into the typewriter or printed out on a computer.

However, envelopes are still used a great deal and the following rules for typing them are fairly simple:

- Start typing halfway down (fig. 29), and one third of the way across. This keeps the name and address well away from post marks and franking machine logos.

- If the words PRIVATE, CONFIDENTIAL, PERSONAL, etc, appear on the letter, they must appear on the envelope to ensure no one other than the addressee (person letter is addressed to) opens the mail. Usually the wording appears above the address, and is separated by a blank line.

- Post towns should be typed in blocked capitals, for example SOUTHAMPTON.

- Postcodes should be on a separate line from the post town, with no punctuation, to enable the Post Office sorting machines to read the codes.

- Postage stamps are affixed to the top right-hand corner of the envelope.

Some envelopes have V-shaped flaps which are a bit of a nuisance when typing. The consistency of your typing will vary because of the hard line the V makes. When you type this sort of envelope, try to avoid the shape of the V and type within it.

Example
'There's something wrong with this typewriter,' Val said to her boss. 'I just can't get it to type clearly on these envelopes. It's OK on headed notepaper. I don't understand it.'

Can you think of a way to improve things, apart from typing in the V?

One way could be to suggest next time new stock is purchased, envelopes with smaller flaps are bought. Or perhaps typing labels and attaching them to the envelopes would help?

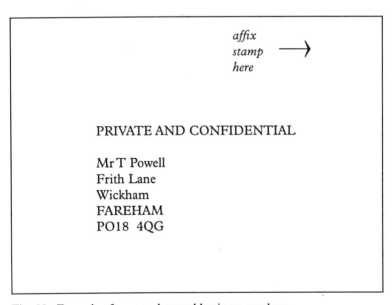

Fig. 29. Example of a properly typed business envelope.

Taking care of your typewriter

Machines need loving care and attention, and a well maintained machine will reward you with years of good service. Treat it gently and remember the following:

- Take care when using Tippex or erasers on electronic typewriters. These clog up the works and cause problems.

- Don't rip paper out of the machine—the force may loosen the rubber roller.

- Don't type unless you have paper in the machine. It leaves carbon on the roller and can damage the rubber.

- Learn how to change the ribbon/lift-off tape properly—don't force them out of the machine. If there is no one to show you, read the typewriter manual. If there is no manual, it will be trial and error. If you do have to force the ribbon cartridge, you are probably doing something wrong. Relax, think about it, and start again.

Example

Assume there is no manual and no one to help you change your typewriter ribbon/lift-off tape. The first thing to do *before* you remove the old one from the machine is to look carefully at the way the ribbon is placed. Most typewriter ribbons are **cartridges**, which makes life a lot easier (they simply clip in), but if they are on two **spools** you will have to write notes (or draw a diagram if you're artistic) of where the ribbon goes. Lift-off tapes can also be very fiddly if they are the spool type. Don't remove these either without making note of how to put them back.

Remove the ribbon first if you are changing the lift-off tape. It will be more difficult to replace it if a cartridge is in your way.

Don't, however, assume your typewriter has a lift-off tape. If you have an older model you may be out of luck and no amount of searching will find one!

Basic typewriter maintenance

Carry out a regular maintenance on your machine as a matter of course:

- Make sure your typewriter is *unplugged and switched off* from the mains electricity first.

- Clean out dust by using a mini-vac (small hand-held vacuum cleaner) or typewriter brush.

- Clean off dirty finger marks from the outside casing using a damp cloth and diluted liquid cleaning agent—*don't allow any liquids to touch the inside or any part of the machine apart from the plastic casing.*

- You may need to use a light machine oil on the print head/ribbon carrier bar. The only movable part of a modern electronic typewriter moves along the shiny metal bar which occasionally dries out. Push the print head to one side. Pour a small amount of oil on a cloth and rub over the bar. Move the print head to the other end of the bar, and do the other side. *Use the oil sparingly— don't drown the cloth.*

Health and safety at work

The typewriter is quite a harmless piece of equipment, and most modern electronic machines are lighter than the older electric or manual models. But you should still consider the following to avoid accidents:

Tips for avoiding accidents

- If you are moving the typewriter, remove the lead or tuck it inside the machine to avoid catching on furniture as you walk past desks and files.

- Bend your knees and keep your back straight when you pick up the machine. Hold it with the heavy side against your chest, ie, keyboard facing away from you. The weight will not pull you forward or strain your back.

- Make sure your destination (desk, table) is clear of obstruction. If you have a heavy machine in your arms, you will have to be a contortionist to clear the area whilst balancing the typewriter on the edge of the desk.

- When plugging into the electricity supply, avoid trailing type-writer leads—they are lethal trip-wires and can cause you dam-age as well as your typewriter.

- If you use an electric or manual model, lock the margins by moving both left and right to the centre of the carriage. This will stop the carriage from shooting off to one side if you tilt the machine.

- Switch off your electric/electronic typewriter and remove the plug from the electric socket at the end of the day.

- Your typing chair should be one where you can adjust the height and back position to suit your specific needs. If you have short legs, a footrest can make life more comfortable.

Summary

1 Follow company layout of documents or to examination standard.
2 Always take a copy of documents.
3 Proof read your own work.
4 Type envelopes with address starting half way down.
5 Include special instructions on envelopes if they appear on letters.
6 Take care of your typewriter and clean it regularly.
7 Remember HASAW.

WORD PROCESSING

The layout of documents in word processing should be the same as for typing. However, processing words using a computer has many advantages including:

- ease of correcting errors
- can spell-check words
- can merge names, addresses, etc, with other documents
- updates documents without the need to retype completely
- can store phrases and paragraphs in its memory.

To get the full benefit from your computer it would pay you to take a course at night school or college if you are new to word processing. Many word processors are very under-used by their operators who only know how to lay out standard letters and how to use basic functions (ie centre, embolden and underscore). There are many more jobs they can do for you . . . if you know what they are capable of!

Two important things to remember when word processing are:

- Never walk away from your computer without **saving** work. You only need to be away for a minute, and all your work could disappear with the flick of a switch (and usually, someone else flicks the offending switch!).

- **Back up** your work onto another disk at the end of the day. Your main work disk could be stolen, lost or damaged—a copy disk will save you many hours of stress as you key in your tenth lost document, kicking yourself for not making a back-up. Store the back-up disk in a different location to the original.

Taking care of your computer

Special fluids can be purchased to clean the screen of your computer, but otherwise the untrained person should leave well alone. Many companies now have maintenance contracts and have their machines regularly checked out by professionals.

Avoid drinking or eating near the computer—keyboards don't like either. Avoid touching exposed sections of computer disks with hands, as small amounts of natural oil can corrupt disks. Don't leave disks in the sun or on the computer—both can damage the disk.

Health and safety at work

The rules for carrying typewriters and care of electric leads should be applied here as well. In addition the following should be remembered when using computers for any task:

- The VDU (screen) is fitted with a **brightness control**, similar to an ordinary television, and should be adjusted for comfort.

- A special **anti-glare screen** can be fitted, which filters out some of the reflection from the screen. If yours doesn't have one and you use the computer a lot, perhaps your boss will get one for you.

- New computers should have **adjustable VDUs** which can be swivelled to a comfortable angle and should be adjusted to a lower level than the operator's eyes. However, many older models don't have such luxuries, but the operator should try to arrange seating and computer at a comfortable level.

- **Document holders** help to avoid eye strain for operators who have to continually look up at the screen from the copy document. If there isn't a holder available, prop a book between VDU and keyboard and place the copy on this, holding it fast with fixing putty.

- In the ideal world, **special work units** for operators incorporate extendable worktops, wide surfaces and all the equipment you need for comfort. However, in the real world you may have to compromise with cushions, blocks of wood (foot rests) and two dcolto puohed together.

- You should **limit the time** you spend looking at the screen. Take a break every now and then just to rest your eyes.

Summary

1 Save your work when you leave your machine.
2 Back up your work disk at the end of the day.
3 Remember HASAW.

DATA PROCESSING

A data processing computer programme is a modern-day filing cabinet. Information is keyed in by an operator, and is sorted and filed by the computer. However, the computer is only as good as the operator who inputs the information. Blaming the computer for lost records and incorrect information is a weak excuse for a badly up-dated database.

If you are unsure of how to use a database, someone will need to get you started. Make notes as you go along—when something is new, it is almost impossible to remember every command unless you have a photographic memory. If there is a manual, keep it by your side for reference. Double-check the information you key in.

Back up copies of your database and always save work before you visit the loo or make a cup of coffee.

DEALING WITH MONEY

Dealing with money will range from petty cash (small amounts of money) to banking the firm's takings. You may not only deal with cash, notes, cheques, postal orders, money orders, but credit cards as well.

Let's deal with the petty cash first.

Petty cash

Most companies, large or small, have a stock of small change—the amounts can vary from £10 to over £100. The money is used to pay for every day items such as milk, tea, postage stamps, and small stationery items. A careful check must be made to ensure the cash is not abused.

Whoever uses the petty cash should supply a **receipt** for what they have bought, as proof of money spent.

● *On no account should you borrow money from petty cash for your own personal use.*

Cash should be kept in a tin or lock-up box and a small note book or a **petty cash ledger** kept with details of money spent. Every time money is taken out or put in, it should be accurately recorded in the book. The actual money in the tin should always add up to the same amount as the balance recorded in the book.

When the cash runs low, more should be obtained from your employer or accountant, and the amount in the tin brought up to the original balance. If you work for a small company, you may have to go to the bank and cash a company cheque yourself.

A petty cash book can be a simple small notebook, or a ledger ruled as in fig. 30.

Whichever type your company uses, the important thing is to keep a check on the cash. If this is your job, ensure the cash tin is in a secure place where no-one will be tempted to help themselves.

Example
You go to the tin and find that the money and the book don't tally. Check your totals again; if they still don't balance, ask other people in the office if they have used any cash from the tin. You may find someone needed a stamp or pint of milk while you were at lunch. Don't scream and shout at them if they have—ask them politely if they could get a receipt next time as you need it for your accounts.

After having a good think yourself, and if no-one else has remembered taking money, check your totals in the ledger book again. You could have miscalculated. If the totals are correct, check the

PETTY CASH LEDGER									
Received 199_	Date	Details	Voucher No	Total Amount	Postage	Office Expenses	Stationery	Sundry	VAT
30.00	9 Dec	Taxi	010	13.50				13.50	
	10 Dec	Stamps	011	2.40	2.40				
	10 Dec	Oil	012	1.40		1.40			

Fig. 30. Extract from a typical petty cash ledger.

amounts on the vouchers to make sure they are the same as in the book.

It may be that someone has taken money and, because of pressure of work, forgotten about it. They may well remember later. But don't do a wall of death—they may be reluctant to tell you if it happens again.

Finally, there is always the possibility (not a pleasant one) that someone may be helping themselves. If you do suspect this, advise your boss, be particularly vigilant with the cash, and try to find a more secure place to hide the tin.

Summary
1 Don't borrow petty cash for your own use.
2 Obtain a receipt as proof of purchase.
3 Get more cash when float is low.
4 Keep records up-to-date.
5 Keep cash secure.

Banking the money

Larger sums of money received in the office have to go somewhere, and they should go into the bank. After dealing with the incoming mail all cheques, cash, postal orders (called **remittances**) should be removed and written into the remittances book and ledger book (or handed to the appropriate person). Cash, cheques, and credit card payments received in the office should also be entered into the remittances book and receipts sent if necessary.

Following this, the remittances should be entered onto a paying-in slip (see fig. 31), supplied by the bank, and banked as soon as possible. Security of money should be observed at all times; never leave money on your desk unsupervised. Put it away in your drawer if you need to leave your desk.

Summary
1 Check amounts.
2 Record in appropriate book/ledger.
3 Send receipt or hand to next person.
4 Fill in paying-in slip.
5 Pay into bank.

HELPING WITH BUSINESS TRANSACTIONS

Business transactions involve buying and selling. Several documents are involved and you may have to help to type/write out invoices (bills), credit notes and monthly statements of accounts.

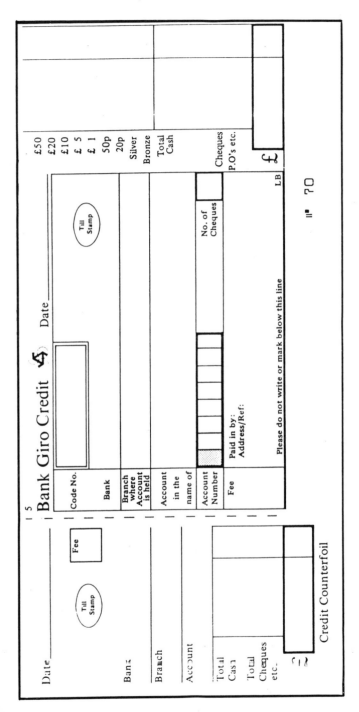

Fig. 31. Example of a paying in slip for a bank.

113

Your maths at school may not have been brilliant, but it doesn't mean you can't calculate invoices, take away discounts and add VAT. You should have a special calculator for working out discount and VAT calculations. If one is not available, these can be purchased quite cheaply from your local stationers or newsagents.

You should know the basic mathematical functions. Remember that discounts are taken off and VAT is added on. The following symbols are used in invoicing:

+	=	add	−	=	subtract
×	=	multiply	÷	=	divide
@	=	at (each)	%	÷	percentage

Some simple calculations
The following simple calculations will help to get you started:

10 × £1.50 =
 6 × £8.60 =

Now calculate the following:

6 boxes of washers @ £1.26 =
12 reels of cable @ £29.60 =

Calculating discounts and VAT
That was easy. Now let's move on to calculating percentages. At the time of publication the VAT rate is 17½%.

Example
Take 18% off £355.20

Key into calculator	355.20
Press	×
Press	18 (the percentage)
Press	%
Total reads	63.936

Therefore, 18% of £355.20 is £63.936.

Round up the final number so your total now reads £63.94 and finish the calculation:

£355.20 −£63.94 = £291.26

To calculate VAT simply change the percentage to 17½% (17.5), ie,
Key into calculator   355.20

Press	×
Press	17.5 (the percentage)
Press	%
Total reads	62.16

To put it all together—fig. 32 is an example of a completed invoice. There is no mystery to invoicing, just basic maths.

SUMMARY

Top ten office duties
1. Answering the telephone and greeting visitors/customers
2. Photocopying and reprographics
3. Mail handling
4. Filing
5. Typing
6. Word processing
7. Data processing
8. Dealing with money
9. Banking
10. Business transactions

OTHER OFFICE DUTIES

That concludes the Top Ten, but it doesn't cover every office skill or task you may be involved in. It would be impossible to detail them all here, but below are a few you may already have some experience with, or may in the future. Again, check in one of the books mentioned in the index should you need further information.

Foreign business transactions
With more and more companies dealing with companies in the EC and other countries, you may need to invoice in currencies other than sterling. This is not quite so daunting as it may first appear. The current **exchange rates** are widely advertised, in newspapers, travel agents and banks. All you have to remember is:

● the rate always refers to £1

Therefore, if the French exchange rate is 7.9, the equivalent English rate is calculated like this:
£1.00 = 7.9 × 1 = 7.9 Francs
£5.00 = 7.9 × 5 = 39.5 Francs
Easy, n'est-ce pas?

INVOICE	No: 029

From:	Dice Services, Frith Lane, Wickham, Hants
Tel:	0489 896238 Fax: 0489 8962231
To:	Bee Videos plc Date: 2 May 199–
	239 Barchester Road
	Shedfield
	Hants
	SO3 2NG

Quantity	Description	Unit	Total
6	Boxes of washers	£1.26	7.56
12	Reels of cable	£29.60	355.20
			362.76
	Less 18% discount		65.30
	Sub total		297.46
	Plus 17½% VAT		52.06
	TOTAL		£349.52
E & OE			

Fig. 32. Example of an invoice. Note: the initials E & OE mean 'Errors and Omissions Excepted'. In other words, if you make a mistake and undercharge (or overcharge), you can correct your error by sending another invoice (or a credit note). Although you should always check your calculations carefully, all is not lost if you *do* make an error!

Taking shorthand dictation

Bram Stoker mentioned shorthand in his famous novel, *Dracula*. Dracula, on seeing the symbols on a letter written by Jonathan Harker, called it a vile thing and an outrage upon friendship and hospitality!

However, it is also extremely handy if you have to take dictation from your employer (or want to write something for your eyes only).

There are several different methods of shorthand. The original, **Pitman New Era**, was superseded by **Pitman 2000** and after, **Pitman Script** and **T-Line**. T-Line appears to be today's favourite and is easier to learn than Dracula's 'vile thing' (which is still used).

If you are working and would like to teach yourself, you need determination and self-motivation . . . and someone to dictate, although this is not essential. Taking down notes from TV or purchasing special shorthand tapes could help you to increase your speeds.

A better way to learn, however, is to enrol at an evening class. This will give you the incentive to practise and your teacher will dictate appropriate passages at carefully timed speeds.

Audio typing

It helps to have good literacy skills if you are asked to type from shorthand or audio recordings. Audio players are rather like small tape players, with the addition of head phones and a control, which allows you to stop and start the tape with your foot, leaving your hands free for typing.

Pay attention to layout and punctuation, as well as to spelling. Your tape is unlikely to have written notes to compare the recording to, and it is your responsibility to produce good, accurate, clean work.

Doing the wages and salaries

Often calculated on computers, this task is usually left to a senior member of staff or wages clerk. Unless you work for a small company, it is unlikely you will be involved in calculating wages.

If you are employed as a wages clerk, you should either have previous experience, or be employed as a trainee. If you are a trainee, your company will arrange for the necessary training.

A wages clerk should be trustworthy and able to maintain confidentiality about other people's salaries. They should keep up-to-date with the latest changes in tax and national insurance contributions, and have good numeracy skills.

Bookkeeping
Good numeracy skills are important for bookkeepers. Attention must be paid to neatness if the bookkeeping is manual (in **ledger books**) as it often is in smaller companies. However, many larger companies now keep their accounts on computers, but attention to detail is still important. One incorrect figure can throw a whole year's accounts out. A mistake involving one penny is often harder to find than a thousand pounds!

Planning journeys
You may have to plan a journey and arrange accommodation. An RAC or AA hotel guide will be a great help with this task. Some computers also come complete with an Autoroute programme, which will work out journeys for you. If you don't have this luxury, you may need an A–Z road atlas.

Arranging meetings
This is usually the job of a senior secretary or personal assistant, but you may be asked to set out a room, organise refreshments and type up agendas. You may also be asked to type up minutes after the meeting.

CASE STUDIES

Lee
'Lee, we have our first training session on BS5750 at the end of the week,' Mr Davenport says, passing him a thick file of A4 paper. 'I need these standards photocopied five times by the end of the day so we can get started on them first thing in the morning.'

Lee takes the pile of papers from his employer. He isn't pleased. 'Must be at least two hundred pages,' he thinks. 'It'll take me ages. He always gives me the crap jobs.' Lee carries on with his word processing, putting off the photocopying until he can face it.

As the day goes on, Lee has put the photocopying to the back of his mind and at 4 o'clock Mr Davenport returns to the office. 'Have you finished the photocopying?' he asks.

Lee's face turns a bright shade of scarlet. He feels as though his throat has completely dried up. As he gasps for air, he mutters. 'I haven't started it yet.'

'Get it done now—and don't go home until its finished!' Mr Davenport is fuming and storms out of the door.

Lee feels like walking out. There's no need for his boss to shout at him like that, but he decides he needs his job, so begins the photocopying. At 5 o'clock he's about to pack up and go home, when Mr Davenport walks in again. 'Where do you think you're going?'

'Home—it's 5 o'clock.'

'I need that work first thing in the morning and your job depends on it. Unless we get the BS5750, you may not have a job next year!'

Lee thinks the BS has something to do with mad cow's disease—he wasn't really listening when Mr Davenport briefed the staff on the new British Standards Quality Control. Without it, they could lose contracts and go out of business.

Chriss

Mr Roberts has just bought a second-hand computer for Chriss to use. 'I thought it would save you time with the accounts and for typing letters. A friend of mine says his does everything.'

'Have you got the manual?' Chriss asks.

'No— I didn't think you'd need one as you've done a course.'

'It was on a different computer. I really will need a manual to get me started on this one. I don't even know which of these disks to use.'

'Sorry, Chriss, but it was such a bargain that I wasn't that bothered about there not being a manual. Can you see if you can get one from somewhere?'

Chriss spends the rest of the day ringing around computer suppliers to see if they can get a copy. She has no luck and finally tries out all of the disks. As one is booting up, she notices the manufacturer's address flash up on the screen. Quickly, she writes it down and sends a letter to them. To her relief, a couple of weeks later a manual arrives. She can now start work on the computer!

Jackie

'Jackie, can you work out the VAT and discount on these invoices and then type them up?' asks Mr Eliot.

'I'm not much good at maths,' she says in a panic. She hated maths at school. She could never understand why anyone would ever want to find the square area of a stupid field if x = y anyway.

'That's no problem,' said Mr Eliot. 'I'll do the first couple for you—if you watch you'll soon catch on'

By the end of the day Jackie had cracked it. She couldn't understand why maths always seemed so hard at school and now so easy at work.

'That wasn't so hard was it? As long as you always double-check your figures you won't go far wrong,' said Mr Eliot after checking Jackie's work. Finding no errors he continues, 'I think I can leave you to do the invoicing on your own from now on.'

Jackie was beinning to feel a lot happier about work. 'I guess I'm not as thick as I thought I was after all!' she said to herself, smiling.

DISCUSSION POINTS

1. What is the point of Health and Safety at Work? Why does Britain bother to have a whole government department geared to health and safety?

2. What is a 'personality clash'? Do you think Lee and Mr Davenport have a personality clash? If so, what could Lee do to change the situation?

3. Why is mail opening one of the most important jobs in an office?

6
Office Job Descriptions

Office job descriptions come in all shapes and sizes—as varied as the types of employer themselves. But here are ten typical office jobs, which can be used as a rough guide:

- office junior
- ledger clerk
- receptionist
- reprographic assistant
- telephonist
- typist/word processor operator
- data processing operator
- clerical assistant
- filing clerk
- audio typist

Such a list can never be complete—the world of work itself is evolving and changing all the time, in response to business needs. But these are quite typical examples, as a glance at the 'situations vacant' in the local newspaper or employment office will show. Let's look at each one in turn.

OFFICE JUNIOR

The office junior will be learning the trade, from the bottom up. Some of the tasks they may be expected to do are as follows:

- answering the telephone and transferring calls
- filing and retrieving documents
- general typing, including invoices, letters, envelopes, etc.
- collecting, sorting and distributing incoming mail
- preparing outgoing mail, including stamping and posting
- photocopying and collating (putting together) leaflets and brochures
- making the tea and tidying up.

LEDGER CLERK

A ledger clerk deals with figures, entering invoices and credit notes, cheques and cash, so he or she needs a good head for practical maths. Clerks don't need to do complicated mathematical equations, but they will need to be able to check figures, add, subtract, divide and multiply—with or without the use of a calculator.

The word **ledger** originates from long ago when candles and daylight were the only form of illumination. Books were balanced on ledges in front of office windows, to take advantage of daylight.

In the 1990s, Ledger Clerks not only have the advantage of electricity, they also have computerised book-keeping facilities. However, many companies still use manual (handwritten) systems, and you should be prepared for this.

RECEPTIONIST

Your main responsibility as a receptionist is to receive visitors, and, often, answer the telephone. You may also be expected to keep the reception area tidy, maintain visitor's registers, take on small typing and other simple tasks, which won't interfere with the main job of dealing with visitors.

If you are interested in this type of position, you will need to be cheerful, of smart appearance, have a clear speaking voice and enjoy meeting people. The impression you give will be important for your company's reputation.

REPROGRAPHIC ASSISTANT

A reprographic assistant has to use not just a photocopier, but perhaps other printing media, such as offset litho. Production of brochures and packaging may be done 'in-house' in large companies and some element of design may come into the job.

A good eye for design would be helpful and some experience in using printing media and perhaps desk-top publishing.

TELEPHONIST

Larger companies employ telephone operators, whose job is to deal with all telephone calls. Usually, the telephonist's job doesn't allow for her/him to take on any other tasks.

Answering the telephone is also a front-line job, and a good telephonist can give customers the impression of a well-run company, efficient and professional. A bad telephonist can lose customers. The bad management of calls can soon irritate and annoy.

The telephonist should have a clear speaking voice and a desire to help the caller.

TYPIST/WORD PROCESSOR OPERATOR

Larger companies employ typist/word processor operators. Generally, a typist has the job of typing letters, envelopes, reports, specifications, and so on.

The typist should be accurate, check work carefully for errors and correct it before handing it back. Accurate spelling is important, as is attention to display of work.

A word processor operator is similar to a typist, but uses a computer to produce the work instead.

DATA PROCESSING OPERATOR

This person keys data into a computer. The computer can't be blamed if there is an error—it can only process information it has been given by its operator.

Operators should be accurate at keying-in-information and capable of checking their own work carefully for errors.

CLERICAL ASSISTANT

Assists with clerical work. This could be in the marketing, buying or personnel department, for example. The clerk would help out with filing, retrieving documents, operating a keyboard, and dealing with paperwork generated in their department.

As for the office junior, the work may be varied and you could be called on to deal with enquiries, sort and distribute mail, prepare outgoing mail and other duties. You will need to be flexible and willing to take on tasks other than those you normally do.

FILING CLERK

The filing clerk's duties would be to ensure files are kept in good order. He/she collects documents from other departments and places them in the correct location. Duties would also include retrieving files requested by staff: 'Could you go and get me the Thompson's work in progress file from Accounts, please?'

A filing clerk needs to work to a system and should ensure papers are filed accurately. Not the sort of job for someone who is easily bored as the work tends to be repetitive.

AUDIO TYPIST

A good grasp of the English language is essential for this type of position as the audio typist will have to type documents from taped dictation. It is important that the person be able to concentrate on their work and will usually work in isolation.

Good proofreading skills are necessary and the audio typist should have a high standard of typing skills regarding document preparation and layout.

There are many other job opportunities available in offices. Fig. 33 gives you some idea of the vast variety to choose from.

OFFICE REFERENCE BOOKS TO HELP YOU

Every office with a telephone should have a copy of the local *Telephone Directory* and a copy of *Yellow Pages*. But what other books should you keep? That really depends on the size of your company and what type of business you work for. Some of the reference books in common use today are listed below and can be used as a guide:

Books to help in the office
ABC Guides for Coach, Bus, Railway, Shipping, Airways
These give times of arrival, departure and destination of travel services. They also give other information, eg, early closing days, fares, etc.

AA and RAC Handbooks
Both books offer services to their members, and in addition, details of hotels and garages in Great Britain (with star ratings), street maps of some towns plus a detailed map of the whole of the country. They also give early closing days in towns and other matters of interest to the traveller.

Black's Titles and Forms of Address
To find the correct form of address, eg how do you address the Queen when she invites you to tea? Look in Blacks.

British Rail timetables
Routes and names of stations together with times of departure and arrival are detailed here. Additional information includes boat services connected to British Rail.

IS THIS YOU?

Temporary clerk

Secretarial assistant   Filing clerk

Marketing assistant

Sales ledger clerk   Wages clerk

Stock control clerk

Office junior   Receptionist

Accounts clerk

Word processing operator   Typist

Data processing operator

Sales clerk   Cost clerk

Credit control clerk

Telephonist   Mailing clerk

Trainee manager

Mail room assistant   Assistant to Transport Manager

Buyer's assistant

Personnel assistant   Secretary

Office machine operator

Design clerk   Production control clerk

Order clerk

Clerical assistant   Buyer's assistant

Company secretary's assistant

Clerk-typist (sales)   Clerk-typist (Personnel)

Cashier

Petty cashier   Office supervisor

Clerk-typist (Buying)

Production assistant   Assistant to Sales Manager

Invoice clerk

Export sales clerk   Telex operator

Purchase ledger clerk

Marketing assistant   Trainee accountant

Despatch clerk

Personal Secretary   Assistant to Training Officer

Reprographic assistant

Customer services assistant   Archives assistant

Fig. 33. Fifty varieties of office work—do you know of any others?

Cyclopedia of Initials and Abbreviations
The meaning of initials and abbreviations are given for words in common use.

Dictionary
One of the most essential books. Gives spelling, meaning, derivation, pronunciation etc of words.

Dictionary of Typewriting
Provides details of how to layout typewritten documents to an acceptable standard.

Euro pages
Names, addresses and telephone numbers of companies in the major EC countries are detailed.

Fax directory
Lists companies and their fax numbers.

Gazetteer
Gives spelling and situation of towns, counties, and so on in Britain.

Guide to British Enterprise
Lists prominent firms in the UK.

Kelly's Directory of Manufacturers and Merchants
Lists manufacturers and suppliers.

Pears Cyclopaedia
A combined dictionary, gazetteer, and ready reckoner. Includes legal data, synonyms and antonyms, etc.

Post Office Guide
Details postal facilities in Great Britain and abroad. Unfortunately, they are very difficult to get hold of now as the last update was in 1987.

Ready reckoner
Answers to calculations involving percentages, discounts, multiplications, etc, can be found quickly using a ready reckoner.

Roget's Thesaurus
Lists words and gives alternatives which mean the same thing.

Telephone directory
Names, addresses and telephone numbers of telephone subscribers. Also included in this section are the *Yellow Pages*, which give trades and professions of subscribers.

Telex directory
Lists telex numbers and answerback codes.

Town guide
Local services and organisations are listed here.

UK Kompass
Names company directors and their companies.

Whitaker's Almanac
Covers world affairs, British and foreign embassies, information about the royal family, cabinet ministers, law courts and an immense variety of other information.

Who's Who
Biographies of famous living people.

Willing's (or Benn's) Press Guide
Lists newspapers and trade journals

Although you may not use all of the above, you may find that several will come in very handy.

Example
Stacey was trying to write a letter for her boss, Bill, but wasn't happy with the draft copy.

> The new design is new and includes a new parts in both the input and output motors.

She has used the word 'new' three times in the first sentence and it sounded very unprofessional.

'I'm sorry, boss,' she said to Bill. 'But I'm just no good at writing—it just sounds so stupid.'

'Here,' Bill replies, passing the *Thesaurus* to Stacey. 'Look up the word you want in the index and see what alternatives it offers.'

Stacey didn't know what a thesaurus was and had never bothered to find out. She was amazed when she checked out the word 'new' and picked several words from the book's list. She then rewrote the sentence, which didn't sound so repetitive:

> The recent design has been updated and includes advanced parts in both the input and output motors.

CASE STUDIES

Lee

After the incident with the photocopying, Lee talked to his parents about his boss. 'I hate him. He gives me all the crap jobs and demands I get them finished before I go home.'

Lee's father worked for the same company and knew Mr Davenport well. He knew he was a fair man and the description Lee gave wasn't the same man!

'Look, son. I'm not so sure you're really cut out for office work. Are you sure it's what you want because it isn't too late to change? Perhaps you'd better have a think about it.'

'I do like working in the office, but my boss picks on me all the time and I'm really fed up.'

'From what I can see,' his father replies, 'I'm not so sure you put a lot of effort into work. You have to remember, you've got to work hard to prove yourself, and you will have to do all the mundane jobs until Mr Davenport is sure you're ready for anything more complicated. I think it's time you pulled your finger out.'

Lee hoped his dad would back him up and was shocked by his reaction. He wanted his dad to speak to Mr Davenport, but it seemed he was on his own. 'Ah well, 'spose I'll have to try again. I know dad—if I blow this job he won't buy me the car he promised me when I'm 17!'

Lee was finally motivated to put some effort into work. The next day he listened to his boss, and carried out his instructions to the letter. And he smiled as he did so. He couldn't believe the change in Mr Davenport, either. For the first time he actually praised him for some work he'd done.

Chriss

'Chriss, can you organise accommodation for me in Birmingham for the beginning of next month. I'm off to the business exhibition and want to stay somewhere near to the city centre.' Mr Roberts turned back to Chriss just before disappearing out of the door. 'Find out the train times as well—I don't fancy driving up there.'

Chriss had never planned a journey before but didn't want to tell her boss. Fortunately, Kevin from the stores came in to bring some paperwork for Chriss. 'What's up, love? Boss gone out and left you again?'

'He wants me to book him accommodation for next week. I'm not really sure where to start.'

'Haven't you got an *RAC Guide*? I've got one in the van you can borrow.' Kevin fetches the book for her and shows her how to use it. 'It gives you all the telephone numbers and addresses, but the rates might be a bit out of date because it's last years copy.'

'Thanks everso,' a relieved Chriss says as Kevin leaves the office. After selecting a couple of hotels, Chriss telephones to find out their rates. After comparing the two, she decides Mr Roberts will probably want to go for the cheaper one and provisionally books it. She'll send a cheque to confirm the booking once she has checked with her boss.

The railway station is only up the road, so she pops up there during her lunch break and collects the appropriate timetables. From the information, she types up an itinerary with all the details Mr Roberts will need to get him to Birmingham. She also types up details of the hotel she has chosen (address, phone number, type of room and room rate) and leaves them on his desk ready for his approval on his return.

Jackie

Jackie is determined to improve her spelling. Her dictionary is always by her side and she has begun to use the *Thesaurus* as well. She has also made herself a small dictionary with words she has difficulty with.

During slack periods in the office, she tests herself on some of the spellings. Mr Eliot notices the effort she is putting into improving herself. 'Would you be interested in taking an evening course in English? The firm will pay for your fees, but you'll have to get there yourself.'

Jackie is keen to have a go. She makes enquiries at the local night schools and is sent several brochures with details of courses.

After studying them with Mr Eliot, she decides to go for her GCSE in English Language. She knows it will be hard work, but she is also beginning to have some ambition and is thinking of her future. As she left school with no qualifications, this could just be the start she missed out on at school.

DISCUSSION POINTS

1   If you are just starting out in the world of work, where do you see yourself in five years time?

2   If you are returning to work after some time, where do you see
    yourself in five years time?

3   Which reference books do you have at home? Which do you use
    more often than the others?

IT'S YOUR FUTURE—DON'T WASTE IT

However you get your first job, don't simply look on work as a way of filling your day and earning a few quid. It is a valuable training ground, and it's a training ground for *your future*.

Don't make a snap decision on day one that you hate the job, that it's boring, that you couldn't possibly spend the rest of yours days in this particular office. It will take you at least a month to get the real feel of an office and to get to know the people you work with.

- be positive

- be realistic

- be open-minded.

Be positive
If you do not feel comfortable at the start of a new job, be positive in trying to fit in. Don't bristle with aggression because no-one has had time to show you everything when you first arrive.

Be realistic
If the office is busy, try to help—but only with things you know you can do. You could waste other people's time by making a mess of something you are unfamiliar with.

Be open-minded
Just because you don't answer the 'phone to begin with, or use the firm's computer, it doesn't mean you never will. You will have plenty of time to try out new things once you have mastered the basic tasks.

Example

Imagine you have left school with an RSA CLAIT (Computer Literacy and Information Technology) Certificate. You like computers and would like to be more involved with them than you are.

For the first month you only answer the telephone, open the mail and do a bit of typing and are getting a bit annoyed at not being able to use the computer. At your interview your future employer had mentioned there would be a chance to go to college to gain more qualifications if you showed that you were capable. But you don't want to wait. You want to use the computer *now.*

You decide it isn't worth staying at the job because you can't ever see things changing. You collect your week's wages on Friday, and never return or 'phone to let them know where you are.

Several months later, you meet a girl you went to school with. She took over your job when you didn't return . . . and she is now at college one evening a week studying for her first computer examination.

How do you think you would feel if this really happened? Do you think it is worth working hard to get what you want instead of giving up too soon?

DOS AND DON'TS

Below are a few 'dos and don'ts' to remember, but there will be many others, and with experience, you could add to the list yourself. To begin with, we will start with the 'do's':

Do's

- **Do** use your initiative and help out when you see someone has a problem, even if it is only to open the door if they are overloaded with files.

- **Do** tidy up behind yourself and make sure your desk is clear at the end of every day.

- **Do** make sure to wash up your own cup—don't leave it to someone else.

- **Do** take note of equipment which needs servicing. If the photocopier breaks when you are using it, make sure to tell someone or 'phone to get it repaired, instead of leaving it for someone else to find.

- **Do** take messages carefully, making sure that all the information is correct.

- **Do** proof-read your work carefully before handing it over to the author.

Don'ts
- **Don't** throw away old documents, or copies of sub-standard work. Cut them up to use as scrap paper for messages and doodles.

- **Don't** expect your boss to proof-read (check for errors) your work. You must do this yourself. Your boss hasn't time to check everything that goes out, and letters sent with errors are a poor reflection on you and the company.

- **Don't** use the telephone for personal calls unless it is urgent. You are not only costing your employer money, but also costing him the time you have spent chatting. If you have an emergency, out of courtesy, ask your boss if you can 'phone home, etc. If he's not around, use your discretion. Avoid lengthy chats with friends. Telephone bills are now itemised and give details of the time the call was made, the number called and how long the call lasted. If you think you can make a sneaky call to your friends . . . be warned—your boss will probably find out!

- **Don't** give out personal information about the people you work with or clients who's files you have access to. It is not only annoying, but, depending on the information, may be against the law.

- **Don't** leave bags, boxes and files where people can trip over them.

LEARNING TO BUDGET

With the excitement of receiving your first week's wages, after paying your housekeeping and bills you will probably blow the rest on a new outfit, a present for your mum or a boxed CD set of your favourite band. However, do think about budgeting your money and perhaps putting some away in a savings account or building society.

Try to get into the habit of saving *some* of your money each week/ month. You may want to buy a car or a new CD player and the worst thing you can do is buy them on hire purchase, extended payments, and so on, where the interest costs mount up at a horrendous rate, and you are saddled with debt.

Banks and building societies make it extremely easy for young people to borrow money—but what happens if you lose your job?

Example
Your company has suddenly gone bankrupt and you are now out of work. You only receive £33 a week from the DSS and, although you have been desperately seeking employment, have found nothing. You have to pay out £130 a month for a car, which sits rusting away in your drive because you can't afford the petrol to run it. You can't afford the payments either, or the insurance, which is nearly £35 a month.

You try to sell the car, but car prices have dropped since you bought it and you are only offered silly money. It wouldn't even cover seven month's payments. You are tempted to take out another loan, over five years, which will make the payments smaller. You have a headache with all the worry.

Finally you decide to sell the car, taking what you can. You write to the finance company to explain your situation, sending them the amount you received for the car. They agree to suspend payments for two months, giving you the chance to get another job. You cancel your insurance and send back your tax disc (which still has six month's tax left). As soon as you receive the money for your car tax, you send that to the finance company.

A cleaner's job comes up at the local factory. You jump at the chance to earn some money. Gradually you pay off your debts and finally manage to find another office job.

You've learnt your lesson the hard way. When you get your pay this time, you put £20 away each week into the building society. You know you'll get another car some day—when you have enough money to pay outright for it. Getting into debt is a mug's game and you don't intend to play it again.

Regular savings

You should get into the habit of saving regularly or you'll end up not saving at all. As they say, don't put off until tomorrow what you should do today, and the first thing you should do when you start work is to open up a savings account. If you think you'll be tempted to take out the money as soon as you've put it in, open an account where you have to give a couple of month's notice to make a withdrawal.

Collect leaflets from the Post Office, Trustees Savings Bank, and building societies. Check out their rates of interest and take your time before deciding which account is the best for you.

Once you have started saving, try to continue. Up the amount if you get a wage increase. Good habits started at the beginning of your working life will be a good grounding for your future.

Pension plan

Some companies offer their own company pension plan, or you could start your own. Usually, pension plans are increased yearly to keep up with inflation. They are paid out on retirement. Premiums are much lower if you start paying early in life, as you have a longer period to pay.

If you decide on starting a pension plan, it would be wise to choose a well-known company. Some of the new, smaller companies have been known to go out of business leaving investors with no money at all. Ask your parents, family friends, or one of the better known banks for independent advice.

CASE STUDIES

Lee

'It's your birthday in two months' time, Lee. Your mum and I have decided to get you a car, but we aren't paying the insurance or tax, so you'd better start saving up for it now.'

'How much do you think it'll cost me, dad?'

'Well, the road tax is over £100 a year and the insurance will probably be at least £300–£400.'

'I didn't realise it would be so much!'

'You could probably pay your insurance montly, but you'll need a bank account to arrange the monthly payments. You've already got a building society account that your mother and I opened when you were smaller. Why don't you put some money in there each week? If you open up a bank account, you could put some in there as well.'

Life was getting a bit complicated for Lee. He wanted the car, but he didn't realise just how much it would cost him. He wrote down everything he had to pay out each week, and with the amount he had left he decided to put three quarters of it away. If he wanted wheels, he guessed he'd better get himself organised.

Chriss

Chriss had always had to budget. Being a single parent wasn't easy. After being with Mr Roberts for three months, he decided to keep her on and gave her a pay rise of £20 a week. She wasn't expecting it at all, and had managed OK on her wage before.

Chriss' wages are paid directly into the bank and instead of spending them, she visited her bank and arranged a standing order to have the extra money paid into her building society. That way she would have a bit of savings and wouldn't have to go to the building society to pay it in each week—the bank would do it for her.

Jackie

Jackie is only earning £29.50 on YT and has to be very careful with her money. She still works at the weekend in the shop and gives her mum the money. She knows if she works hard Mr Eliot may take her on permanently at the end of her time, so she is prepared to keep working for the low wages.

As well as attending night school, she also goes back to college once a week to work towards office skill examinations. By the end of her two years on YT she will be well qualified.

After six months at work, Mr Eliot is so pleased with her he takes her on 'employed status'. This means she still has the advantages of YT, but she gets extra money from Mr Eliot.

Instead of telling her mum about her pay rise, she decides to open up a savings account and religiously puts the extra money in each week. She feels a bit guilty about deceiving her mum but she wants to have some money of her own and her mum isn't very good at saving. If she knew about Jackie's extra money she would only use it to buy more cigarettes or drink. Jackie doesn't indulge in either and so she keeps the matter to herself.

SUMMARY

- Be positive in your approach to work.

- Be realistic about what you are capable of.

- Be open-minded where work is concerned.

- Assess your own performance and make improvements where necessary.

- Consider opening a savings account or pension scheme.

POINTS FOR DISCUSSION

1   Have you ever done something, for example mowed the lawn,
    washed up, and knew you hadn't done it properly? Did you
    decide to do it better the next time—trim the edges of the lawn,
    dry up as well and put the crockery away? Or did you feel pleased
    with your performance because now you wouldn't be asked to do
    it again?

2   Have you ever saved money? Do you see any point in putting
    money away, or do you think it a waste of time, and believe in the
    motto: 'you can't take it with you, so why save?'

3   Do you believe you are too young to think about a pension?

8
The Office of the Future

Finally, let's look at the office of the future. Will it be so different to the one of today? One thing is for sure, job security isn't something we can take for granted in the 1990s. All employers have to look at ways of cutting costs.

FROM HOT DESKING TO NEW TECHNOLOGY

One new idea is **hot desking** or the **virtual office** where more than one employee shares the same desk space. Employees who spend time away from the office take their lap-top computers with them. On their return, they off-load information from their 'portable office' and communicate with colleagues doing the same.

Working from home

Many people now work from home, with their computer their only colleague. Some homeworkers receive their instructions and communicate via the VDU/telephone and contact with other staff is limited. Other homeworkers collect or have delivered material to be typed/word processed and are usually paid by the number of words typed. The employer saves office and desk space, time and money.

New technology

New technology is without a doubt beginning to change the face of the office, with businesses, large or small, installing computers for word processing and data processing. This trend will certainly continue.

Networking

Some schools, colleges and larger organisations are already networked together, receiving their mail electronically via telephone or cable lines, and communicating regularly with each other using computers. Work keyed in at one end of the country can be received by another computer at the other end, within seconds.

Faxes and phones

Faxes, capable of sending exact replicas of pictures, diagrams and documents are in common use today, and small concerns as well as large regularly use them.

The telephone, too, is leaping into the future. *Star Trek* led the way: British Telecom has followed on with the introduction of the **videophone**. For about the same cost as a video recorder, a set of two 'phones can be purchased and installed into an ordinary telephone line. A two-way conversation can be held with the participants smiling (or scowling) at each other across the air waves. The cost of a call is the same as a conventional voice call.

THE HUMAN FACTOR

But, despite all the modern technology, the office as we know it will still be in existence for many years to come. The main ingredient in the office which cannot be replaced by machine is man/woman—and we are not quite ready to dehumanise the office completely.

Today, training is high on the list for employers, and help via television, training courses, books and videos is readily available. The emphasis is on successfully **managing** people and **communicating** with colleagues and customers. The investment in people would be pointless if we were all to become isolated individuals operating in our own small room with only a computer for company. It would be a sad day if we couldn't share a problem with a colleague over a cup of tea at break time.

Here's hoping your own future career in the office will be successful, and that this book will encourage you to assess and improve your performance all the time.

After all, *you* are the future and good staff are still difficult to find!

Checklists of Office Skills

NATIONAL VOCATIONAL QUALIFICATIONS (NVQs)

The following checklists cover units issued by the lead body for Business Administration. They are nationally recognised standards and qualifications, based on skill and the ability to do a job (National Vocational Qualification = NVQ). Examining bodies such as RSA, Pitman, City and Guilds, use them as their guidelines.

To ensure NVQs keep ahead of current demands in today's office, there will inevitably be changes in the future. The standards detailed here can be used well into 1995 and will work alongside new standards implemented in 1994 (Administration 1, 2, 3 and 4).

The checklists may use words you don't understand. Some of these can be found in the glossary with an explanation of their meaning. You may need to check a dictionary for others not listed.

Summary

Filing
1.1   File documents and open new files
1.2   Identify and retrieve documents

Communications
2.1   Process incoming and outgoing business telephone calls
2.2   Receive and relay oral and written messages
2.3   Supply information for a specific purpose
2.4   Draft routine business communications

Typing/word processing
3.1   Produce typewritten alpha/numerical information
3.2   Identify and mark errors on typed material for correction
3.3   Update records in a computerised database

Book keeping
4.1   Process petty cash transactions
4.2   Process incoming invoices for payment

Office supplies
5.1   Issue office materials on request and monitor stock levels

Mail handling
6.1   Receive, sort and distribute incoming/internal mail
6.2   Prepare for despatch outgoing/internal mail

Reprographics
7.1   Produce copies from original documents using reprographic equipment

Communications
8.1   Receive and assist callers
8.2   Maintain business relations with other members of staff

Health and safety at work
9.1   Operate safely in the workplace

Communications
10.1   Creat and maintain professional relationships with staff
10.2   Create   and   maintain   professional   relationships   with customers

Information handling
11.1   Respond   to   customers'/clients'   specific   request   for information
11.2   Inform   customers/clients   about   available   products   and services
12.1   Maintain an established filing system
12.2   Supply information for a specific purpose
13.1   Process records in a database
13.2   Process information in spreadsheets
13.3   Access   and   print   hard   copy   reports,   summaries   and documents

Telephone calls and messages
14.1   Process telephone calls using multiline/switchboard system
14.2   Transmit and transcribe recorded messages
14.3   Transmit and receive copies of documents electronically

Reception
15.1   Receive and direct visitors
15.2   Maintain reception area

Business document production
16.1   Produce business documents from drafts
17.1   Produce business documents from recorded speech (audio typing)
18.1   Produce business documents from dictated material

Arranging travel and accommodation
19.1   Make travel arrangements and book accommodation
19.2   Arrange meetings involving three or more people

Bookkeeping
20.1   Make and record petty cash payments
20.2   Receive and record payments and issue receipts
20.3   Prepare for routine banking transactions
20.4   Make payments to suppliers and others
21.1   Reconcile incoming invoices for payment
21.2   Prepare and despatch quotations, invoices and statements
21.3   Process expenses claims for payment
21.4   Order office goods and services
22.1   Process documentation for wages and salaries
22.2   Process direct payment of wages and salaries
22.3   Arrange credit transfers
23.1   Maintain cash book, day book and ledger records

1.1. File documents and open new files within an established filing system

Standard to aim for

Can you . . .? Do you know . . .?

File all documents in correct place and order without delay

Store all materials safely and securely without damage

All documents sorted and filed correctly

Refer to appropriate person if unsure of where documents are filed

The importance of correct and accurate filing?

How to classify documents?

Sort, handle and store documents skillfully?

Stick to organisation procedures regarding special/confidential files and know policy for keeping files?

Filing and indexing systems eg, alphabetical, geographical?

Understand company files and how to classify documents?

Filing methods, eg, vertical, lateral, box files, etc?

File without delay and plan/organise work within deadlines?

1.2. Identify and retrieve documents from within an established filing system

Standard to aim for

Can you . . .? Do you know . . .?

Requested documents are found, retrieved and passed to correct person without delay

Staff are notified of delays in supplying files and reasons politely explained

Records of file movements are up-to-date and legible

How company system works and understand classification of files?

Classify files?

Organisation rules regarding special/confidential files and policy for keeping files?

Filing and indexing systems?

Filing methods?

Booking out and brought forward systems?

Plan, work and organise yourself within deadlines?

2.1. Process incoming and outgoing business telephone calls

Standard to aim for	*Can you . . .? Do you know . . .?*
Calls are answered within four rings using correct company introduction	Use telephone directories?
	Listen, understand, ask for and write down relevant information?
Name of caller and their requirements are correctly obtained	Speak and write clearly?
	Messages are written correctly with all necessary information?
Callers are politely answered and/or transferred to appropriate person if necessary	Use equipment properly, and know how to plug in?
	Charge rates and costs?
	Use of telephone directories?
Caller only given disclosable information	Your own company and its products and services?
	Style of greeting to callers as used by own company?
Dial out using correct number and make contact with appropriate person	Appropriate paperwork to be completed to confirm details, ie, letter, order etc?
State clearly the purpose of the call	Security, safety and emergency procedures?
Faults with the telephone are reported immediately to the appropriate person	Importance of working well with colleagues and clients, establishing good relationships?

2.2. Receive and relay oral and written messages

Standard to aim for	*Can you . . .? Do you know . . .?*
Obtain all relevant information courteously	Communicate effectively, orally and in writing?
	Establish rapport and goodwill with colleagues and clients and understand why necessary?
Verify with callers	Listen and interpret information?
Messages passed to person/location	Use effective questions to check understanding and to seek additional information?
Communicate relevant information accurately	Use appropriate tone, style, vocabulary?
	Compose accurate and relevant notes?
	Know own organisation structure, location, responsibilities of staff?

Standard to aim for   *Can you . . .? Do you know . . .?*

Know departmental responsibilities?
Understand procedures for passing information?

2.3. Supply information for a specific purpose

Standard to aim for   *Can you . . .? Do you know . . .?*

Correctly identify and access relevant sources of information

Abstract, list and classify appropriate data correctly

Supply information to appropriate person within required deadlines

Report difficulties in achieving targets promptly and politely—explain reasons why

Interpret oral and written instructions?

Liaise effectively with colleagues and others?

Use dictionaries and other reference books?

Plan and select presentation styles?

Spell and punctuate correctly?

Compose notes, letters?

Plan and organise work within deadines?

Use information sources (eg manual files, computer files, books, lists, microfiche, viewdata, etc)?

2.4. Draft routine business communications

Standard to aim for   *Can you . . .? Do you know. . .?*

Letters and memos are drafted within specified deadlines and are legible and contain all essential information

Communications are drafted and presented in an approved format

Plan and select presentation styles?

Use correct spelling and punctuation?

Compose grammatically correct sentences?

Use appropriate business English and English grammar?

Use dictionaries and other reference books?

Construct letter/memo using correct 'rules' for letter writing?

Importance of context in which letters are written?

Identify needs of person receiving letter?

Access information from correct sources?

Organisation rules regarding styles, formats, vocabulary and signatories?

3.1 Produce typewritten alpha/numerical information

Standard to aim for

Can you . . .? Do you know . . .?

Produce 150 words or numeric equivalent in 10 minutes with no more than 2 uncorrected typing or spacing errors

Corrections are clean and unobtrusive

Security and confidentiality of work is always maintained

Machine faults are dealt with by using instruction manuals and/or reporting promptly to someone in charge

Maintain machinery and carry out regular care and routine checks—including diagnosing faults?

Operate and use keyboard layout?

Use fingering techniques?

Use correct posture/seating position?

Understand oral and written instructions?

Plan layout of work?

Correct errors using proper technique?

Use dictionaries/reference books/glossaries?

Save information, as appropriate?

Print document and use correct instructions?

3.2. Identify and mark errors on typed material for correction

Standard to aim for

Can you . . .? Do you know . . .?

Correctly identify all errors in typed work

Check and identify all numerical data for errors or omissions

Mark clearly all data/text to be corrected

Script conforms to correct layout specified

Uncertainty in any work is reported and changed as directed

Use correct spelling and punctuation?

Use dictionaries and other reference books?

Use calculator correctly and effectively?

Use correct techniques for checking work, ie, two readers, use of ruler, etc?

Correctly mark work with proper correction signs?

Erase and correct using appropriate methods?

Use approved organisation styles and formats?

3.3. Update records in a computerised database

Standard to aim for	*Can you . . .? Do you know . . .?*
Access correct field every time	Read and interpret manufacturer's and/or organisation's instructions?
Understand and enter correct data into appropriate fields	Read and interpret manuscripts with uneven quality of writing?
	Operate safety procedures and care of equipment?
Always maintain security and confidentiality of information	Use computer keyboard and operating systems?
	Take care of equipment?
Report and accurately describe faults/failures and symptoms promptly	Use styles and formats as per organisation format including naming of files?
	Back up disks and maintain security procedures?
Follow operating and safety procedures at all times	Input data using correct format?
	Common system faults and symptoms?
	Plan and organise work within deadlines?

4.1. Process petty cash transactions

Standard to aim for	*Can you . . .? Do you know . . .?*
Handle cash securely and always follow safety procedures	Use a calculator to ensure financial calculations are correct?
Transactions are accurate, and recorded and supported by correct, authorised petty cash vouchers	Complete simple forms/records?
	Use petty cash systems, including proper use of recording procedures and who to gain authorisation from?
Report irregularities promptly to an appropriate authority	

4.2. Process incoming invoices for payment

Standard to aim for	*Can you . . .? Do you know . . .?*
Identify all discrepancies between invoices and delivery notes	Communicate effectively orally and in writing?
Identify all errors in invoice charges	Know what documents and recording methods your organisation use and how to deal with invoices correctly?
Promptly report all discrepancies and errors	What the purchasing, sales and accounts departments do?
Pass forward for payment correct and authorised invoices only	Importance of confidentiality?
Up-to-date records are legible and accurate	Use a calculator to ensure financial calculations are correct?
	Complete simple forms/records?

5.1 Issue office materials on request and monitor stock levels

Standard to aim for	*Can you . . .? Do you know . . .?*
Requests for stock are actioned promptly and accurately	Count amounts and estimate requirements?
	Use a calculator effectively?
Handle and store stock safely at all times	Check quality and condition of materials/equipment?
	Complete simple forms/records?
	Issue and record stock using correct systems?
Carry out stock checks and reconcile inventory as directed, reporting any shortages/damage	Types of materials stored and approximate amount used over given period?
	Minimum and maximum stock levels and procedures for emergency reordering?
Report promptly any discrepancies on incoming deliveries checked against orders	The location and proper storage of material?
	The procedures for storing and handling hazardous materials, eg thinners, etc?
Legible and accurate records of stock movements are up-to-date	Laws relating to receipt of goods? Use correct stock control procedures, includes dealing with damaged/obsolete stock?

6.1. Receive, sort and distribute incoming/internal mail

Standard to aim for   *Can you . . .? Do you know . . .?*

Standard to aim for	Can you . . .? Do you know . . .?
Receive deliveries of mail and report any damaged/suspicious items to appropriate authority	Use letter opening equipment?
	Recognise unusual or suspicious looking items?
Check all mail to ensure enclosures are securely attached and report missing items promptly	Sort and attach enclosures to documents?
	Sort and distribute documents to correct person?
Always follow security procedures for cash and valuables	Use calculator correctly for financial calculations?
	Complete simple forms and records?
Open mail as directed ensuring no damage occurs to contents	Plan and organise work within deadlines?
	Structure, location and responsibilities of other people in your organisation?
Sort and deliver all mail to correct location within laid down time schedules	Organise lists to circulate documents?
Report promptly any unavoidable delays in distributing to appropriate person	Procedures and systems your organisation use for dealing with all categories of routine, incoming and outgoing mail?
	The reporting procedures for dealing with suspicious, dangerous or damaged packages?

6.2. Prepare for despatch outgoing/internal mail

Standard to aim for   *Can you . . .? Do you know . . .?*

Standard to aim for	Can you . . .? Do you know . . .?
Check documents for signature and enclosures. Identify and rectify any missing items	Use Post Office guides and take information from reference books?
	Select suitable sized envelopes, packets, parcels and wrapping materials?
Securely seal in appropriate size envelope, packet or parcel all items for mailing	Weigh and measure using imperial and metric?
	Use scales and franking machine?
Address all mail legibly	Use calculator correctly for financial calculations?

Calculate and apply correct postal rates

Post Office sorting requirements, collection and postal deadlines are met

All records are up-to-date, legible and accurate, and filed correctly

Follow security procedures at all times (stamps, money, etc)

Complete simple forms and records?

Plan and organise work within deadlines?

Understand correct procedures and systems for dealing with all outgoing mail?

Standard Post Office procedures, guides and services?

Express delivery services and who agencies are?

7.1. Produce copies from original documents using reprographic equipment

Standard to aim for

Produce correct copies within required deadlines

Keep paper wastage to a minimum

Place all pages of documents in correct order

Pages of document are neatly and securely fastened together

Distribute all copies/originals correctly within required deadlines

Identify faults and deal with according to manufacturer's instructions

Promptly report unforeseen difficulties in achieving targets—politely explain reasons why

Follow operating, recording and safety procedures at all times

Can you . . .? Do you know . . .?

Read and interpret instruction manuals?

Interpret oral and written instructions?

Recognise and distinguish suitable and unsuitable documents for copying?

Recognise equipment malfunctions?

Complete simple forms and records?

Understand operation and routine care and maintenance of commonly used reprographic equipment/material?

Different fastening methods, eg, binding, staplers, clips, etc?

Recognise numbering systems and ensure correct sequence of pages?

The procedures for re-ordering materials?

Relevant costs of various reprographic methods and understand Copyright laws?

8.1. Receive and assist callers

Standard to aim for	Can you . . .? Do you know . . .?
Greet all callers promptly and courteously and find out their needs	Listen to and interpret information? Recognise and react appropriately to body language signals?
Give only disclosable information to callers	Communicate orally to good effect? Rules on security and confidentiality of information and security of the building?
Direct and/or escort all callers to destination, as required	Structure of your organisation and know the location and responsibilities of the people who work there?
Explain politely reasons for delay/non-availability of assistance	Operate and know the telephone system?
Situations outside the jobholder's area of responsibility are identified and assistance promptly requested	Deal with difficult/aggressive visitors and know where to get help if necessary? Correct greeting style(s) used by the organisation?

8.2. Maintain business relations with other members of staff

Standard to aim for	Can you . . .? Do you know . . .?
Respond willingly to requests from colleagues	Structure, location and responsibilities of other people in organisation?
Explain clearly and politely where requests from colleagues cannot be met	Liaise and communicate effectively with peers and senior colleagues? Understand oral and written requests?
Discuss and, where possible, resolve difficulties encountered in working relationships	Plan and organise work within deadlines? Dress, act and behave to the organisation's standard?
Refer accurately to an appropriate person any difficulties you cannot sort out yourself	Understand importance of establishing good communication and goodwill with colleagues and clients?

9.1. Operate safely in the workplace

Standard to aim for	*Can you . . .? Do you know . . .?*
Keep your own working area free from hazards	Read and interpret instructions?
	Recognise and deal with potential hazards?
	Causes of hazards and accidents in an office environment?
Ensure all equipment used is operated safely as laid down in instructions	Use safe working practices including good housekeeping?
	Communicate orally to good effect?
	Complete simple forms and records?
Potential hazards to the well-being of yourself and others are recognised, rectified and/or reported promptly to an appropriate person	Use safe lifting and carrying techniques for moving machinery/equipment/materials?
	Operate safely and take care of equipment?
	Safety policy, safety rules and reporting and emergency procedures in the organisation?
Report accidents promptly and record accurately in accordance with legal and/or organisation's policy	Where fire fighting equipment is kept, how to use it for different types of fire?
	Locate and activate alarms?
	Locate first aid equipment and fill in register?
	Who qualified first aiders and safety representatives are—where to locate them?
	Know why safety legislation is important?

10.1. Create and maintain professional relationships with other members of staff

Standard to aim for	*Can you . . .? Do you know . . .?*
Act promptly and willingly where possible to action requests from colleagues within the jobholder's responsibility	Communicate and liaise with colleagues effectively?
	Plan and present information?
Pass essential information on to colleagues promptly and accurately	Understand oral and written messages?
	Plan and organise work within deadlines?

When required, politely ask for assistance

Make arrangements regarding division of work and joint responsibilities effectively and in agreement with others

Discuss, resolve or report accurately to an appropriate person any significant difficulties in working relationships

Pay attention to dress and appearance—keep to your organisation's standard?

Behave in a responsible manner?

Structure, location and responsibilities of other people in your organisation?

Use organisation's internal telephone system?

Be aware of your own and employer's responsibilities under the Health and Safety at Work Act?

10.2. Create and maintain professional relationships with customers and clients

Standard to aim for

Promptly and politely greet all customers and clients

Acknowledge known customers/clients by name in an appropriate, friendly manner

Conduct conversations with customers/clients in manner which promotes goodwill and trust. Take into account work and time pressures, needs of other customers/clients

If knowledge or job responsibilities are exceeded, direct promptly and politely customers/clients to the appropriate authority in a professional manner

Promptly, accurately and willingly action policies, procedures and activities to promote customer/client trust, satisfaction and goodwill

Politely explain reasons for any delays/non-availability

Can you . . .? Do you know . . .?

Communicate effectively (oral and written) with specific emphasis on conversational skills?

Deal with difficult customers/clients?

Recognise and respond to non-verbal communication signals?

Handle complaints, including organisation policy and procedures?

Dress and ensure appearance to organisation standards?

Company policy on disclosure of information?

Use greeting styles used by organisation?

Legal obligations to the public and aware of Public Liability and Trade Descriptions Act?

11.1. Respond to customers/clients specific requests for information on products/services offered by the organisation

Standard to aim for	*Can you . . .? Do you know . . .?*
Deal promptly and politely with all customer/client enquiries	Communicate effectively (oral or written)?
Ensure requests for privacy are respected and interviews are conducted in a manner which maintains confidentiality	Deal with difficult/aggressive/distressed customers or clients? Recognise and respond to non-verbal communication signals? Interpret oral and written information?
Check and record accurately all customer/client details relating to their eligibility to request information	Write summary reports? Use interview skills? Locate and layout written materials?
Identify promptly where you are unable to help and refer the matter to higher authority	Regulations/instructions concerning eligibility of requests for information?
Match benefits of products/services to particular client circumstances	Policy on disclosure of information for your organisation?
Ensure calculations are correct	Greeting styles used by your organisation?
All interview records are accurately completed and agreed actions carried out	Legal implications of Public Liability and Trade Descriptions Act on your organisation?

11.2. Inform customers/clients about available products and services

Standard to aim for	*Can you ...? Do you know ....?*
Greet customers promptly and politely—identify their needs	Interpret oral and written requests? Use listening and questioning skills?
Describe features, advantages and benefits of products/services and match with relevant client needs	Recognise and respond to non-verbal communication signals? Deal with difficult/aggressive customers/clients?
Access and make available all relevant information to customer/client within optimum time scales	Use computer and paper based sources of information (files etc)?

Relevant information not available is explained and an alternative arrangement for access agreed with customer/client

Requests for information and/or advice outside of job holders responsibility are promptly passed to an appropriate authority

Note and re-order shortages of writing materials as defined in organisation policy

Locate and layout written material?

Re-order stationery?

Products and services currently on offer?

Policy on disclosure of information for your company?

Greeting style/s used by your organisation?

How the Trade Descriptions Act affects your organisation?

How the Financial Services Act affects your organisation (if appropriate)?

12.1. Maintain an established filing system

Standard to aim for

Can you ...? Do you know ....?

Control and record all file and document movements accurately

Maintain all documents in good condition and in correct location

Identify all overdue files/documents and know/operate organisation's system for their return

Open new files in accordance with established system and mark/identify them legibly

Identify, take out and deal with all out-of-date documents as directed

Always maintain security and confidentiality of information

Always follow safety procedures

Understand and identify systems used and know how to classify documents?

Complete simple forms/records?

Be methodic when sorting, handling and storing documents?

File using indexing and cross-reference systems?

Procedures and systems of organisation, including special and confidential, and policy for retaining files?

Filing methods, ie, lateral, vertical, computer-based etc?

Operate equipment, ie, shredders, etc?

Use circulation lists and know why they are used?

Book out and bring forward files?

Relevant aspects of the Data Protection Act?

12.2. Supply information for a specific purpose

Standard to aim for	*Can you ...? Do you know ...?*
Correctly identify and access information sources	Liaise effectively with colleagues and others?
Abstract all relevant information	Use reference material effectively, eg, computer files, books, lists, etc?
Options and alternatives are identified and offered where resourced information does not match defined needs	Interpret oral and written instructions?
	Present information, eg, graphs, charts, diagrams, etc?
Select suitable display format for intended purpose	Use language effectively, ie, in spelling and punctuation?
Transcribe and compile all data correctly	Compose notes, letters, memos, etc?
Present all essential information within required deadlines	Plan and organise work within deadlines?

13.1. Process records in a database

Standard to aim for	*Can you ...? Do you know ...?*
Ensure all data files conform to defined specifications	Interpret oral and written instructions (manuals, variable quality manuscripts etc)?
Create, amend and delete new datafiles correctly and as directed	Use a keyboard?
Accurately transcribe and enter data into correctly identified fields	Understand business terminology?
	Plan and organise work within deadlines?
Ensure all database files are without transcription error	Plan/match wanted formats with available software/hardware?
Always back up files produced and store safely	Proof-read screen and printed documents?
Locate, access and retrieve requested information within specified time constraints	Operate safely, care/maintain equipment (include knowledge database capability)?
Ensure security and confidentiality of information is always maintained	Security and back-up procedures?
Identify and report faults/ failures promptly	The styles and formats of organisation, including file naming?
	Use formulae?
Always follow operating and safety procedures	Relevant aspects of Data Protection Act?

13.2. Process information in spreadsheets

Standard to aim for

Can you . . .? Do you know . . .?

Ensure spreadsheet formats conform to defined specifications

Create, amend and delete spreadsheets correctly as directed

Transcribe and enter data into correctly identified files without error

Files always backed-up and stored safely

Projections are correctly generated as directed

Maintain security and confidentiality of information at all times

Identify and report faults/ failures promptly

Follow operating and safety procedures at all times

Interpret oral and written instructions from manuals and manuscripts of varied quality?

Use a keyboard?

Business terminology?

Plan and organise work within deadlines?

Plan and match formats with available software/hardware?

Proof-read screen and printed documents?

Operate safely, maintain/care for equipment (include knowledge of database capability)?

Secure and back-up your work?

Styles and formats of organisation, including naming files?

Use formulae?

13.3. Access and print hard copy reports, summaries and documents

Standard to aim for

Can you ...? Do you know ....?

Correctly access document/record/field to locate information as directed

Conform all printed output to specifications

Collate and distribute documents correctly as directed

Always maintain security and confidentiality of information

Identify and report faults/ failures promptly

Always follow operating, safety and maintenance procedures

Interpret oral and written instructions (from manuals, etc)?

Diagnose print problems?

Operate safely, care and maintain equipment?

Call documents onto screen?

Common print methods and types of printers?

14.1. Process incoming and outgoing telephone calls using a multiline or switchboard system

Standard to aim for

Can you ...? Do you know ....?

Use approved organisation manner to answer calls promptly and clearly

Identify callers and their requirements

Transfer incoming calls correctly or take messages and promptly pass them on

Correctly obtain external telephone numbers and establish required contact

Identify and offer options/alternatives where specific requests cannot be met

Use courteous and helpful manner at all times

Describe and promptly report system faults accurately

Operating and safety procedures are followed at all times

Structure, location and responsibilities of people in organisation?

Operate and use the facilities of telephone system?

Use British Telecom directories, codes and internal directories correctly?

Ensure cleaning and hygiene routines are carried out?

Communicate effectively with colleagues and others (including listening to and interpreting information?

Policy and procedures on security, safety and emergencies (bomb threats, etc)?

Appreciate the costs in relation to system used?

14.2. Transmit and transcribe recorded messages

Standard to aim for

Can you ...? Do you know . . .?

Transcribe recorded messages accurately and identify/prioritise urgent messages

Promptly pass on messages in order of priority

Compose and record instructions ensuring timed announcements give accurate information

Promptly report identified faults

Always follow operating and safety procedures

Operate and use an answering machine correctly?

Structure, location and responsibilities of people in your organisation (including procedures for passing on information)?

Interpret written instructions in manuals, etc?

Listen to and interpret information including written messages?

Project your voice?

14.3. Transmit and receive copies of documents electronically

Standard to aim for	*Can you ...? Do you know ...?*
Copies despatched and received are always acceptable quality	Use a keyboard?
	Policy, procedures and styles used by organisation?
Despatch accurate material only	Operate and use installed equipment and facilities?
	Use dictionaries and other reference books effectively, eg, UK and foreign directories?
Transmit all outgoing material to correct destination according to instructions	Interpret written instructions, eg manuals?
	Interpret and verify oral and written instructions and messages?
Deliver all incoming material promptly to correct location	British Telecom/other suppliers and obtain new codes, numbers, answerback codes and information update?
Legible and accurate records are up-to-date	Make effective use of language, eg, spelling, grammar?
	Use accepted abbreviations and contractions?
Promptly identify and report faults Always follow operating and safety procedures	Routine maintenance and cleaning procedures for installed equipment?
	Plan and organise work within deadlines?

15.1. Receive and direct visitors

Standard to aim for	*Can you ...? Do you know ....?*
Greet all visitors promptly and courteously	The structure, location and responsibilities of people in organisation?
Identify visitors' names and needs	State policy and procedures of organisation of greeting visitors, security, safety and emergencies?
Only give disclosable information to visitors	How to take messages and where they are passed to?
Direct and/or escort visitors in accordance with organisation's policy Politely explain reasons for any delay/non-availability of staff	Telephone systems and operation?
	Use information sources correctly?
	Deal with difficult/aggressive visitors, ie, recognise and react

Keep legible and accurate records and ensure all are up-to-date

Promptly pass on accurately recorded messages to correct location

Always follow security and safety procedures

appropriately to physical communication signals?

Give visitors information on available car parking arrangements?

Communicate effectively, both orally and in writing?

15.2. Maintain reception area

Standard to aim for

Can you ...? Do you know ....?

Keep reception area tidy and free from hazards

Update and clearly display notices and displays—keep in good condition

Always neatly display publicity and other reading materials and ensure they are up-to-date

Always ensure essential directories are available

Keep reception area attended in accordance with organisation's policy

Policy and procedures of organisation on maintenance of reception area, including display of notices?

Request stationery and know where publicity and other materials can be obtained?

Use effective communication, (oral or written)?

Liaise effectively with colleagues and others?

Compile and maintain organisation charts and internal directories?

Methods and techniques of information display?

Be responsible for self, colleagues and visitors regarding health, safety and security?

Reception design

16.1. Produce a variety of business documents from handwritten/typewritten drafts

Standard to aim for

Can you ...? Do you know ....?

Use keyboard correctly?

Practice housekeeping?

Produce 1,200 words in a 2.5 hour working period with no more than 8 uncorrected spacing or typing errors

Always produces backup and/or hard copy files and store safely

Safely operate, care and maintain equipment?

The correct stationery sizes and qualities?

Proofread screen and print documents?

Styles and formats both organisational/conventional?

Amend documents accurately as directed

Ensure layout conforms to organisation house style and/or accepted typing conventions

Any corrections are unobtrusive

Put together and deliver copies/originals/printouts correctly as directed

Always maintain security and confidentiality of information

Promptly identify and report faults

Always follow operating, safety and maintenance procedures

Business terminology and English grammar?

Use dictionaries, reference books, glossaries, etc?

File systems and indexing principles?

Interpret oral and written instructions including manuals?

Read and transcribe variable quality manuscripts and drafts?

Plan and organise work with deadlines?

Plan layout of work in a variety of formats?

Explain the benefits and limitations of typewriters and word processing equipment?

17.1. Produce a variety of business documents from recorded speech (audio typing)

Standard to aim for

Produce 600 words in 1.5 hour working period with no more than 4 uncorrected spacing or typing errors
Correctly interpret and implement all recorded instructions
Layout conforms to organisational house style and/or accepted typing conventions
All corrections are unobtrusive
Correctly collate and route copies/originals as directed
Always maintain security and confidentiality of information
Identify and report faults promptly
Always follow operating,
safety and maintenance procedures

Can you ...? Do you know ....?

Transcribe variable quality recorded material containing insertions (sometimes misleading) and corrections?

As Unit 16

Use audio equipment and know safety and hygiene rules?

Co-ordinate audio equipment with typewriter?

Agree audio standards and organisation specifications?

18.1. Produce a variety of business documents from dictated material (shorthand dictation)

Standard to aim for

Can you ....? Do you know ....?

Transcribe all information from notes dictated at a minimum speed of 70 wpm

As Unit 16, plus . . .

Identify, check and rectify uncertainties in text

Produce approximately 375–400 words in 1 hour working period with no more than 3 uncorrected spacing or typing errors

Detail knowledge and use one of the shorthand systems?

Layout conforms to organisation house style and/or accepted typing conventions

Develop shorthand vocabulary, short forms and phrases?

All corrections are unobtrusive

Collate and route copies/ originals correctly as directed

Use listening and memorising techniques?

Always maintain security and confidentiality of information

Identify and report faults promptly

Always follow operating, safety and maintenance procedures

19.1. Make travel arrangements and book accommodation

Standard to aim for

Can you . . .? Do you know . . .?

Accurately plan/make arrangements reflecting specified requirements consistent with organisational policy

Access and use information sources effectively, eg, timetables, hotel guides, car hire, maps, exchange rates, visas/vaccinations, agencies?

Common travel constraints, eg, delays, surcharges, etc?

Identify and report alternatives where specified requirements cannot be met

Arrange travel documents, ie, passports, travellers cheques, foreign currency, etc?

Confirm and record all agreed arrangements and costs

Use a calculator correctly to calculate British currency in relation to foreign?

Compose letters of confirmation?

Present all necessary documents in good time together with details and arrangements

Booking procedures and structure of allowances used in organisation?

Use a telephone effectively both nationally and internationally?

19.2. Arrange meetings involving three or more people

Standard to aim for

Can you . . .? Do you know . . .?

Check availability of participants and facilities against proposed meeting date(s)

Confirm date of agreed meeting and arrangements to be made

Inform participants of arrangements in advance of meeting

Despatch all necessary papers to participants in advance and/or provide copies at meeting as directed

Always maintain security and confidentiality of information

Communicate effectively (oral or written), including using the telephone?

Identify requirements and calculate costs?

Structure, location and responsibilities of people in organisation?

Use information sources effectively, ie, directories, reference books, timetables, hotel guides, etc?

Local suppliers and services, caterers, visual aid hire, car parking, etc?

Organisation procedures for booking meeting rooms?

Types of meeting and meeting protocol, including documentation?

20.1. Make and record petty cash payments

Standard to aim for

Can you ...? Do you know ...?

Accurately record and support all transactions by correctly authorised petty cash vouchers

Accurately record cash withdrawals from main cash account

Investigate and promptly refer or resolve all queries

Always follow cash handling security and safety procedures

Accurately balance as directed cash and petty cash book records

Always follow confidentiality procedures

Petty cash systems, including recording procedures and who authorises transactions?

VAT guidelines?

Calculate finances, including using a calculator?

Reconcile cash to records?

Communicate effectively, ie orally and in writing?

Ensure security in relation to cash handling and storage?

Complete petty cash vouchers?

Benefits of using an imprest system?

20.2. Receive and record payments and issue receipts

Standard to aim for

Can you ...? Do you know ....?

Count cash and give correct change where applicable

Correctly verify cheque and credit card payments prior to acceptance

Correctly complete and issue all receipts

Identify and deal with all discrepancies in accordance with laid down procedures

Follow security procedures at all times

Legible and accurate records are up-to-date

Methods of storing cash, ie, till, terminal and/or cash drawer?

Handle cash using different techniques, ie, counting, giving change, etc?

Use calculator for financial calculations including discounts, etc?

Communicate effectively, oral and written?

Complete forms and records?

Operate credit card imprinters?

Security and safety arrangements for handling money?

Procedures and documentation used in organisation?

VAT guidelines?

20.3. Prepare for routine banking transactions

Standard to aim for

Can you ...? Do you know ....?

Complete all paying-in and withdrawal documents correctly

Ensure all money calculations are correct

Always follow security procedures Identify and deal with all discrepancies in accordance with laid down procedures

Records are up-to-date, legible and accurate

Correctly complete financial calculations, including use of calculator?

Complete forms/records?

Plan and organise work within deadlines?

Use banking services and procedures, arrangements and documentation?

Security arrangements for money, including storage and variations of time/day?

Procedures and documentation used in organisation?

Foreign currencies and currency exchange?

20.4. Make payments to suppliers and others

Standard to aim for

Can you ...? Do you know ...?

Check all payment requests for accuracy and authorisatlon

Correctly complete financial calculations, including use of calculator?

Identify and report promptly all discrepancies and/or errors

Complete cheques and counterfoils?

Complete forms and records?

Correctly prepare all cheques

Reconcile invoices, credit notes and statements?

Plan and organise work within deadlines?

Accurately prepare remittance advice—despatch with payment

Procedures and recording systems/ documentation used in payment organisation?

Authorised payments are despatched to correct recipient, location within defined time constraints

Authorisation procedures?

VAT guidelines?

Allowable discounts?

21.1. Reconcile incoming invoices for payment

Standard to aim for

Can you ...? Do you know ...?

Identify and report all discrepancies between invoices and delivery notes

Identify and report all errors in invoice charges

Operate and use manual and computerised accounting systems?

Functions of purchasing, sales and accounts department?

Rectify as directed, all discrepancies and errors

Procedures and documentation used in organisation, including importance of confidentiality?

Only pass correct and authorised invoices forward for payment

Use price lists and interpret, including delivery charges, VAT guidelines, discounts?

Operate filing systems?

Investigate and report, or resolve, all queries

Correctly complete financial calculations, including using a calculator?

Legible and accurate records are up-to-date

Communicate effectively, oral and written?

Only disclose information to authorised persons

Plan and organise work within deadlines?

21.2. Prepare and despatch quotations, invoices and statements

Standard to aim for

Can you ...? Do you know ....?

Use agreed information correctly for all preparatory calculations

Correctly prepare all quotations, invoices and statements, and despatch to correct recipients/destination

File/distribute correctly all copies of documents

Always deal with enquiries and complaints in accordance with organisation's procedures

Records are legible, accurate and up-to-date

Information is disclosed only to those persons authorised by organisation's policy

Operate and use manual and computerised accounting systems?

Functions of purchasing, sales and accounts departments?

Procedures and documentation used in organisation including importance of confidentiality?

Interpret and use price lists, including delivery charges, VAT guidelines, discounts, etc?

Use filing systems?

Correctly complete financial calculations, including use of calculator?

Communicate effectively, oral and written?

Plan and organise work within deadlines?

21.3. Process expenses claims for payment

Standard to aim for

Can you ...? Do you know ....?

Identify and investigate all errors in expenses claims

Promptly report any unresolved discrepancies and errors

Pass for payment only authorised and correctly completed expenses claims

All records are up-to-date, legible and accurate

Always maintain security and confidentiality of information

Organisation codes and practice for dealing with reimbursement of expenses, including special and non-routine payments?

Taxable/non-taxable expenses?

Effective communication, oral and written?

Correctly complete financial calculations, including use of calculator?

21.4. Order office goods and services

Standard to aim for	*Can you . . .? Do you know . . .?*
Despatch all letters of enquiry to potential suppliers conveying precise specified requirements	Purchasing procedures of organisation, including order processing/ emergency orders?
	Sources of supply, catalogues, price lists?
Correctly complete and despatch to selected supplier(s) all order forms	Types of materials/services used?
	Documentation of stockable and special items?
Maintain stocks at agreed levels	Relationship between imperial and metric units?
	Organisation policy on quantity, quality, cost?
Records are up-to-date, legible and accurate	Correctly complete financial calculations, including estimating future requirement levels based on demand/ availability?
	Collect, classify and compare relevant information? Communicate effectively, oral and written?

22.1. Process documentation for wages and salaries

Standard to aim for	*Can you ...? Do you know ...?*
Calculate gross pay correctly from appropriate documentation	Correctly complete financial calculations, including using a calculator?
Correctly calculate statutory and voluntary deductions using standard tables and reference books	Interpret information, ie, clock cards, tax tables, NI tables and reference books?
Correctly prepare pay slips, identify gross and net pay within required deadlines	Complete forms/records?
Statutory and other records are up-to-date, legible and accurate	Use manual and computerised payroll systems?
Accurately complete and despatch within required deadlines all returns	Plan and organise work within deadlines?
Handle pay queries with tact and courtesy	Statutory and voluntary deductions (including year end procedures and other statutory returns)?
Identify and deal with all discrepancies in accordance with organisation procedures	Banking/Building Society procedures (ie, BACS)?
Maintain confidentiality of information at all times	Procedures and documentation used in the organisation
	Rules governing confidentiality?

22.2. Process direct payment of wages and salaries

Standard to aim for

Correctly prepare and issue wage packets within required deadlines

Always follow security procedures

Records are up-to-date, legible and accurate

Deal promptly and courteously with wage queries

Always maintain confidentiality of information

Can you . . .? Do you know . . .?

Ensure security procedures for cash handling/paying out wages are carried out?

Banking procedures and documentation?

Procedures and documentation used in organisation including non-routine occurrences?

Correctly complete financial calculations, including using a calculator?

Complete forms/records?

Rules governing confidentiality?

22.3. Arrange credit transfers

Standard to aim for

Correctly prepare credit transfer slips within required deadlines

Correctly complete bank schedules

Deal with all queries promptly and courteously

Identify and deal with all discrepancies in accordance with laid down procedures

All records are up-to-date, legible and accurate

Only disclose information to authorised persons

Can you ...? Do you know ....?

Correctly complete financial calculations, including use of calculator and currency exchange?

Complete forms/records/summaries?

Plan and organise work within deadlines?

Banking services, procedures, arrangements and documentation?

Procedures and documentation used in organisation?

23.1 Maintain cash book, day book and ledger records

Standard to aim for

Can you ...? Do you know ....?

Accurately record details of all cash income and expenditure in Cash Book

Accurately record details of all goods and services received in credit in Purchases Day Book

Accurately record details of all goods and services supplied in credit in Sales Day Book

Support all entries by correctly authorised primary documentation

Transfer totals from primary records to the correct ledger (nominal/real)

Totals and balances are correct

Identify and report promptly all discrepancies to correct authority

Accurately prepare from ledgers VAT returns, age debt analysis and customer/ supplier statements

Principles of double entry book-keeping?

Systems for describing and categorising purchases and sales under a variety of headings?

Use manual and computerised accounting systems?

Procedures and documentation used in organisation?

Different types of ledger-based systems?

VAT guidelines?

Correctly complete financial calculations, including use of calculator?

Communicate effectively, oral and written? Compare and interpret numerical information from difference sources?

Plan and organise work within deadlines

Answers to Mail Handling Questionnaire

1 What is a remittance?
   A = Money received, either a cheque, postal order or cash

2 How would you deal with Private and Confidential mail?
   A = Deliver it to the person it is addressed to—unopened

3 Why should you date-stamp all mail?
   A = If there is a query, you can check the date it was received.

4 If a letter is delivered to you but is addressed to another company, what would you do with it?
   A = Re-post it

5 Can you name two things which show that something has been enclosed with a letter?
   A = The word Enc or Encs at the bottom of the page, or three full stops typed in the margin

6 What do you write in a Remittances Book?
   A = Details of any monies received in the mail

7 What details appear on an organisation chart?
   A = Company departments and who works in them

8 What do the initials HASAW stand for?
   A = Health and Safety at Work

9 What is a paying-in slip used for?
   A = Paying in remittances to the bank

10 What should you do before throwing envelopes away?
   A = Double-check they are empty

Glossary

abstract—to take out, ie, to take information out of a file

access—to call up or get into a computer database or file to find information

BS5750—British Standard quality assurance. Recognises a standard of quality in a company's systems performance

classifying documents—deciding which name/number it is best to file a document under, ie, alphabetical under name, numerical under reference number

communicating—to 'talk' to another person by word of mouth, telephone or by written/typed words

competent—having qualifications or skills in a task

copyright law—the law designed to stop people from publishing/copying material written/produced by someone else without the author's permission

correspondence—writing of letters, memos, and so on

counselling—to talk over a problem and by discussing, help to offer a solution

cultivate—to develop a skill or task by practice or training

curriculum vitae—list of personal details, work experience, and qualifications

data—information

discrepancy—disagreement/doesn't agree with other information

effectively—being able to produce or accomplish a task correctly

environment—your surroundings—at home, work, and so on

familiarisation—getting used to a skill or task by practice or training

fanning paper—separating sheets of paper by making them fan out. Requires practice to make the fan

initiative—taking the first step

interpret—to read and make sense of/understand

interview techniques—knowing the correct way to act at an interview

inventory—detailed list of equipment or resources (eg, paper, typing ribbons, pens)

irregularities—things which are against the rules or out of normal order

keyboarding skills—knowing how to use a typewriter/computer keyboard correctly

legible—can be read easily and understood clearly

legislation—relating to the making of laws

liaise—to talk or work together with others for a purpose

literacy—the ability to read and write

non-verbal communication—expressing yourself without speaking, ie, frowning, smiling, angry expression

numerate—the ability to add, subtract, divide

peers—equal working partners

personal hygiene—take responsibility for your appearance and cleanliness

personal qualities—your good points, ie, honesty, good time-keeping, reliability

personally effective—the ability to show that you are a good worker, by good timekeeping, hard work, taking on responsibilities

potential—anything that may be possible

reconcile—to agree or adjust and bring into settlement

recruitment officer—the person who decides whether you are suitable for a job or not

relevant—connected to the subject

remittance—an amount of money in cash, cheque, postal order

resolve—to solve a problem

self-motivated—able to work without being pushed by other people

tactful—being able to do or say the right thing at the right time

training allowance—an amount of money paid while you work and train towards qualifications

trial period contract—a work contract for a limited time. Could vary from a month to six months. Gives employer and employee time to see if they suit each other

verbal—by word of mouth

verify—to establish as true by checking evidence

vocational qualifications—qualifications gained by using your work experience as proof of being able to do a job

Further Reading

Book-keeping Made Simple, Geoffrey Whitehead (Macmillan Education).

Discover Book-keeping and Accounts, David Spurling (Pitman Publishing).

How to Be a Freelance Secretary, Leonie Luzak (How To Books).

How to Manage Computers at Work, Graham Jones (How To Books).

How to Master Book-Keeping, Peter Marshall (How To Books).

How to Master Business English, Michael Bennie (How To Books).

How to Pass That Interview, Judith Johnstone (How To Books).

How to Start a New Career, Judith Johnstone (How To Books).

Information Processing, Elaine Mullins (Pitman Publishing).

Mastering Office Practice, Paul Bailey (Macmillan Education).

Office Procedures, John Harrison (Pitman Publishing).

Secretarial Procedures, Helen Harding (Pitman Publishing).

Typewriting Dictionary, Pamela Bennet (McGraw Hill Book Co).

Universal Typing, Edith Mackay (Pitman Publishing).

Index